GERMAN GRAMMAR REVISION

Kernpunkte

CW00953699

VICTOR JOHNSON

Nelson

Contents

Introduction; grammatical terms; dictionaries

PART IV — VERB FORMS AND TYPES

PART IX — VERBS IN CONTEXT

PART X — HINTS ON TRANSLATION OF PARTICULAR WORDS

INTRODUCTION

GRAMMATICAL TERMS

Definite Article — the

Indefinite Article — a

Noun — names a person or thing; e.g. boy, apple.

Gender — In German a noun is:

	MASCULINE	FEMININE	NEUTER
(the . . .)	der Mann	die Frau	das Mädchen
	der Tisch	die Flasche	das Buch
(a . . .)	ein Mann	eine Frau	ein Mädchen
	ein Tisch	eine Flasche	ein Buch

Note: Gender is not necessarily linked to sex.

Number — whether singular or plural:
the man/the men (der Mann/die Männer)
the woman/the women (die Frau/die Frauen)
the child/the children (das Kind/die Kinder)

Cases — There are 4 in German:

1) **Nominative or Subject** — the 'doer'
(except in the passive; see Section 35a)
The boy kicks the ball. = *Der Junge* schlägt den Ball.
Note: Every sentence *must* have a subject.
2) **Accusative or Object** — the receiver of the action or thought.
The boy kicks *the ball*. = Der Junge schlägt *den Ball*.
I like *the salad*. = Ich mag *den Salat*.
3) **Genitive** — translates 'of'.
The *girl's* father = The father *of the girl* = Der Vater *des Mädchens*
4) **Dative or Indirect Object** — 'to', 'for'.
He gives *the child* the book. = the book *to the child* = Er gibt *dem Kind* das Buch.
She cooked *me* lunch. = lunch *for me* = Sie kochte *mir* das Mittagessen.

Apposition — a noun which tells more about a previous noun is described as being *in apposition*.

We spent the night in a village, *a nice little place* near a lake.
Here 'a nice little place' is in apposition to 'a village'. In

German the noun in apposition takes the same case as the noun to which it refers:

Wir übernachteten *in einem Dorf, einem schönen Örtchen* in der Nähe eines Sees.

Pronoun — substitute for a noun.

Types of Pronoun:

1) **Personal** — Indicating a person:

I $\left.\right\}$ you $\begin{array}{l} \text{he} \\ \text{him} \end{array}\left.\right\}$ $\begin{array}{l} \text{she} \\ \text{her} \end{array}\left.\right\}$ $\begin{array}{l} \text{it one someone} \\ \text{nobody} \end{array}$ $\begin{array}{l} \text{we} \\ \text{us} \end{array}\left.\right\}$ $\begin{array}{l} \text{they} \\ \text{them} \end{array}\left.\right\}$

me

2) **Interrogative** — Introducing a question:
who? what?

3) **Possessive** — Indicating possession:
mine, yours, his, hers, ours, theirs.

4) **Relative** — Relates or connects two parts of a sentence:
The vandals *who* smashed the windows were caught.
The cake *that* I ate was delicious.
The coin *which* he found turned out to be valuable.

5) **Reflexive** — where the action is done to the subject:
I wash myself — He washes himself — You wash yourselves

Adjective — Describes or tells more about a noun:

a *red* coat   *some* coats

Types of Adjective:

1) **Attributive** — If the adjective comes *before* the noun.
An *old* coat

2) **Predicative** — If the adjective comes *after* the noun.
The coat is *old*.

3) **Possessive** — *My* coat, *your* coat, *his* coat
indicating ownership

4) **Demonstrative** — *This* coat, *that* coat, *some* coats.
pointing to something or someone

5) **Interrogative** — *Which* coat? *What* sort of coat?
in a question

Verb — The 'doing' word:
I eat   I sing   Go!

Infinitive of the verb — to do something:
to eat, to sing
or after 'I can', 'I must':
I can go.

Person

1st person singular — I *go*
2nd person singular — you *go*
3rd person singular — he, she, it, one, the car, woman etc. *goes*

1st person plural   — we *go*
2nd person plural   — you *go*
3rd person plural   — they, the cars, people etc. *go*

Agreement (of Subject and Verb)
Singular Subject → Singular Verb
Plural Subject   → Plural Verb
3rd person singular subject → 3rd person singular verb *ending*

Impersonal Verbs — Used only in the 'it' form:
It is raining.

Tense — e.g. Present — I go.
Future — I shall go.
Past — I went.
Conditional — I would go.

Imperative — A command:
Eat it!

Active — The subject is the 'doer':
The family is watching television.

Passive — The subject has something done to it.
(or him or her):
The dog is being fed.

Regular or 'Weak' Verbs — which in English, for instance, to form
the Past Tense just add 'd' or 'ed':
I love → I loved
and add 'te' in German:
ich liebe → ich liebte

Irregular or 'Strong' Verbs — have their own special forms in the Past
Tense:
I fly — I *flew* (ich fliege — ich *flog*)
and sometimes in the Present Tense:
I am, you are, he is (ich bin, du
bist, er ist.)

Transitive and intransitive — A transitive verb has a direct object:
Verbs I cooked *the eggs*.
An intransitive verb has no direct
object:
The dog barked.
Some verbs can be used transitively or
intransitively:
The co-pilot flew the plane
(*transitive*)
He flew (*intransitive*)

Adverb — Tells more about a verb, an adjective or another adverb:
He walks *slowly* (says more about a verb)
She looks *very* old (says more about an adjective)
He is *surprisingly* well informed (says more about another
adverb)
Adverbs are of three types:
Time   Manner (= how)   Place (= where)
He *always* drives *slowly*   *there*

Preposition — word or words 'preposed' or put before a noun or pronoun,
usually describing time, place or manner:
After five o'clock

In front of the door
Near me

Conjunction — A joining word which connects what would otherwise be
separate sentences:
I did not know *whether* he would come.

Sentence — A group of words (or possibly even one word) which contains
a verb, and which makes complete sense:
I run the race.
I run.
Run! (The subject 'you' implied)

Clause — A part of the sentence with its own verb. The following sentence
has four clauses:

If I see him tomorrow/I shall tell him/that he must study
hard/until he has mastered the basic facts.

Main Clause   — A clause which makes complete sense on its
own; in the sentence above the main clause is:
I shall tell him.

Subordinate Clause — A clause which does not make complete sense
in itself. In the sentence above the subordinate
clauses are:
If I see him tomorrow
that he must study hard
until he has mastered the basic facts

Direct Statement and Question — what is/was actually said, usually
between inverted commas or speech
marks:
"I'm coming"
"Where are you going?"

Indirect Statement and Question — or reported speech, in a subordinate
clause:
He said *that he was coming*.
He asked *where you were going*.
"Can you tell me *when the train comes
in*?"

Syllable — A word or part of a word pronounced with a single effort of the
voice:
dog — one syllable
chicken — two syllables
supercalifragilisticexpialidocius — fourteen syllables

DICTIONARIES

Buying a Dictionary

Check that any dictionary being considered
1) gives plurals of nouns
2) has a strong verb list
3) indicates verbs taking sein in the Perfect and Pluperfect
4) gives clear distinctions between different senses of a word — indication
   for instance with 'grow' of the difference between *wachsen* (= get bigger)
   and *werden* (= become)
It is also very helpful when it is indicated in the main word list that the verb
is irregular and the irregular forms themselves are listed, at least for the
simple verbs without prefixes. *Harrap's Concise German and English
Dictionary* covers all these features.

Using a Dictionary

Before saying "The word isn't in"
1) If it is a verb with a prefix, remove it: *verlief* → *lief*. Then try looking up
   the verb form *lief*, but if you can't find it (only the most recent and most
   helpful dictionaries include irregular forms as normal entries), look for
   lief in the strong verb list, and you will find it is the past tense of *laufen*.
   Now you can look up the full infinitive *verlaufen*.
2) If it is a compound noun which is genuinely not listed, divide it up into
   its component parts, remembering that there is often an *s* added in the
   middle:
   Staatschef = *Staat* + *Chef* (there is no such word as *Schef*!)
   It is also possible there will be an *n* in the middle, as in *Eichenholz* which
   is made up of *Eiche* ('oak') and *Holz* ('wood'), or the first part of the
   word may be a plural form, e.g. *Hühnerei* made up of *Hühner* which is
   the plural of *Huhn* ('hen') and *Ei* ('egg'). Once you have identified the
   words which form the compound look up any you do not know and it
   should not be difficult to work out the meaning.

PART ONE — NOUNS

§1 TABLE OF REGULAR NOUNS

SINGULAR	Masculine	Feminine	Neuter
Nominative	der Vater	die Dame	das Kind
Accusative	den Vater	die Dame	das Kind
Genitive	des Vaters	der Dame	des Kindes
Dative	dem Vater	der Dame	dem Kind
PLURAL			
Nominative	die Väter	die Damen	die Kinder
Accusative	die Väter	die Damen	die Kinder
Genitive	der Väter	der Damen	der Kinder
Dative	den Vätern	den Damen	den Kindern

§2 CASES (see also introduction)

A) **Nominative case** is required both before and after sein (to be), and **werden** (to become).

> Das ist **mein** Wagen.   Er wird **ein** alter Mann.

B) **Accusative case** is required after **haben** and all verbs with a direct object.

> Ich habe **einen** Sohn.   Sie wirft **den** Ball.

C) **Genitive case** indicates possession. **Note:**

(i) A masculine or neuter singular noun takes an ending.

(ii) A one syllable noun usually adds **es**:
des Mannes   of the man   eines Hause**s**   of a house

(iii) A noun of more than one syllable adds **s**:
des Gartens   of the garden   eines Mädchens   of a girl
Remember genitive noun ending by:
short noun → long ending **es**
long noun → short ending **s**

(iv) **Note:**
Feminine singular and *all plural* nouns have no genitive ending:
der Frau   of the woman   der Männer   of the men
so: **des/eines** means genitive ending on noun
der/einer means no genitive ending on noun

(v) *Absence of apostrophe with Genitive Name*
Unlike English, German mostly omits the apostrophe:
Paul's book = **Pauls** Buch
The apostrophe only appears in German after an **s**, **tz** or **z** at the end
of the name:
Hans' Buch **Moritz'** Buch **Heinz'** Buch

D) Dative case — In addition to translating 'to' and 'for':

Er gibt **dem Kind** ein Geschenk.
He gives the child a present.
Das spart **mir** Zeit.
That saves me time.

the dative case is used with the sense of 'from':
Sie nahm **ihrem Sohn** das Buch.
She took the book from her son.

§3 NOUNS WHICH DECLINE IN MOST CASES

A) Some masculine nouns in German take endings in all cases other than
nominative singular:

(i) Der Junge, der Herr, der Polizist, der Kunde, der Mensch, der
Matrose.

(ii) Some words taken from other languages, e.g. der Präsident,
Student, Pilot, Soldat.

(iii) Some animals, e.g. der Affe, Bär, Elefant, Löwe.

(iv) Nationalities, e.g. der Däne, der Russe, der Schwede.

The endings are **en** or (if the word already ends in **e**) **n**:

	SINGULAR	PLURAL	SINGULAR	PLURAL
Nom.	der Junge	die Jungen	der Polizist	die Polizisten
Acc.	den Jungen	die Jungen	den Polizisten	die Polizisten
Gen.	des Jungen	der Jungen	des Polizisten	der Polizisten
Dat.	dem Jungen	den Jungen	dem Polizisten	den Polizisten

B) Note specially **der Herr** which takes **n** in the singular but **en** in the
plural

i.e. der Herr   die Herren
      den Herrn   die Herren
      des Herrn   der Herren
      dem Herrn   den Herren

C) Note: The following masculine nouns not only take **n** in all cases except the Nominative Singular; they also take an extra **s** in the Genitive Singular:

der Gedanke	des Gedank**ens**
der Glaube	des Glaub**ens**
der Name	des Nam**ens**
der Wille	des Will**ens**

D) Finally note the declension of **das Herz**:

das Herz
des Herz**ens**
dem Herz**en**
Plural throughout — Herz**en**

§4 GENDER OF NOUNS

In most cases the gender must simply be learnt, but there are some useful guidelines and rules.

MASCULINE are

A) Male persons and animals

der Mann   der Arbeiter   der Koch
der Elefant   der Schwan   der Bär
(but note **das** Männchen = cock bird/male animal, neuter because a diminutive — see below)

B) Words from verbs saying what someone or something does, ending in **-er**

der Arbeiter   worker   der Schalter   switch   der Beschleuniger accelerator

C) Seasons, months, days and points of the compass

der Sommer   der Mai   Montag der 24. Mai   der Norden

D) Words ending in **-ling**

der Fremdling   der Frühling

FEMININE are

A) Female persons and animals

die Frau   die Arbeiterin   die Köchin   die Elefantin
die Henne   die Bärin
(but note **das** Weibchen = hen bird/female animal and **das** Mädchen/**das** Fräulein = girl, neuter because diminutives — see below)

B) Most nouns ending in **-e**

die Socke   die Länge
(but note exceptions **der** Gedanke   **der** Name   **der** Wille
der Käse   **das** Auge   **das** Ende   **das** Interesse   **das** Gemüse and
many other nouns beginning with **Ge-**)

C) Nouns ending in **-heit, -keit, -schaft, -tät, -ung, -ur, -in, -ion, -ei, -ie**
and **-ik**

die Freiheit   die Schwierigkeit   die Freundschaft   die Majestät
die Kleidung   die Diktatur   die Studentin   die Automation
die Konditorei   die Energie   die Logik

NEUTER are

A) words ending in **-nis, -tel** and **-tum**

das Geheimnis   das Viertel   das Eigentum

B) Diminutives (words giving the sense 'small') usually ending in **-chen** or
-lein

das Händchen   little hand   das Männlein   little man
However **Mädchen** and **Fräulein** are used for girls of any size.

C) Infinitives of verbs used as nouns

das Lernen   das Reisen   das Essen   das Leben

Note: Two nouns placed together to form one noun (a compound) take the
gender of the last noun:
        der Brief + die Marke → **die** Briefmarke
        die Hand + das Gepäck → **das** Handgepäck

§5 PLURALS OF NOUNS

A) General rules

(i)   A masculine one syllable noun adds **e** and an umlaut (¨) if possible
       on the vowel (only **a, o, u,** and **au** can take an umlaut → **ä, ö, ü,**
       äu):
        der Gast → die Gäste
        der Freund → die Freunde (never umlaut **eu**)

(ii) A neuter one syllable noun adds **er** and an umlaut if possible:
        das Haus → die Häuser
        das Kind → die Kinder

(iii) A feminine noun adds **en** or just **n** if it already ends in **e**:
        die Tür → die Türen
        die Pflanze → die Pflanzen
        If it ends in **-in**, the plural has an extra **n**:
        die Freundin → die Freundinnen

(iv) Masculine and neuter nouns of more than one syllable ending in **-el**, **-en** and **-er** add nothing except an umlaut where possible:
    das Viertel → die Viertel
    das Mädchen → die Mädchen
    der Bruder → die Brüder

(v) Nouns ending in **-nis** double the **s** and add **e**:
    das Geheimnis → die Geheimnisse
    die Kenntnis → die Kenntnisse

(vi) Masculine nouns ending in **-ist** and **-ent** add **-en**:
    der Polizist → die Polizisten
    der Präsident → die Präsidenten
    See also §3A) above.

(vii) Only foreign words take **s** in the plural:
    Café**s** Disco**s** Hotel**s** Kamera**s**
    Karton**s** Kino**s** Restaurant**s** Tramp**s**

Other nouns not coming under previous headings? Look them up in a dictionary.

Note: With the exception of foreign words whose plural ends in **s**, the dative plural of the noun must end in **n**. If it does not do so already, add **n**:
    die Gäste *but* dative den Gäste**n**

B) Common exceptions to the above plural rules

Masculine — Arme Busse Hunde Männer Schuhe Tage Vettern Wagen Wälder

Feminine — Hände Kühe Mütter Nächte Städte Töchter Wände Würste

Neuter — Betten Hemden Jahre Ohren Pferde Schafe Schweine

C) Further points to note

(i) Das Wort has two plurals:
    Worte (connected words in a text)
    Wörter (unrelated words)

    Er konnte es nicht mit **Worten** ausdrücken.
    He could not put it into words.
    Im Wörterbuch sind 100 000 **Wörter**.
    There are 100,000 words in the dictionary.

(ii) Die Bank has two plurals:
    die Bank (= seat, bench) → die Bänke
    die Bank (= bank) → die Banken

(iii) Nouns singular in German:
    die Brille (*pair of*) spectacles
    die Hose (*pair of*) trousers (*plural* Hosen *also used*)
    die Schere (*pair of*) scissors
    die Waage (*pair of*) scales

(iv) Nouns plural in German:

Halsschmerzen	sore throat	('throat pains')
Kopfschmerzen	headache	('head pains')
Magenschmerzen	stomachache	('stomach pains')
Zahnschmerzen	toothache	('tooth pains')

(v)

das Gemüse	vegetables (*already plural in sense, so no plural*)
das Obst	fruit (= *fruit generally, so no plural*)
das Gebäude	building → *plural* die Gebäude
der Kopfsalat	lettuce → *plural* die Salatköpfe
der Saal	big room, hall → *plural* die Säle

(vi) die Polizei ('police'), die Familie ('family'), die Menge ('crowd'), die Gruppe ('group') are singular nouns requiring a singular verb:
Die Polizei kommt.   Die Familie ißt.   Die Menge ruft.   Die Gruppe wandert.

PART TWO — THE BASIC FIVE TABLES OF GERMAN AND ADJECTIVES

§6 I & II — ARTICLES

I DEFINITE ARTICLE ('THE')

	Masc.	Fem.	Neuter	Pl.
Nom.	der	die	das	die
Acc.	den	die	das	die
Gen.	des	der	des	der
Dat.	dem	der	dem	den

der/die/das-words
(i.e. words declining like **der/die/das**):

dieser — this
jener — that
jeder — each, every
welcher — which
solcher — such
mancher — many a

N.B. neuter sing. nom. and acc. endings -**es** not -**as**, e.g. dies**es**, jen**es**

II INDEFINITE ARTICLE ('A', 'AN')

	Masc.	Fem.	Neuter
Nom.	ein	eine	ein
Acc.	einen	eine	ein
Gen.	eines	einer	eines
Dat.	einem	einer	einem

ein-words
(i.e. words declined exactly like **ein** in the singular and taking the same adjective endings in the singular):

kein, mein, dein, sein, ihr, unser, euer, lhr, ihr.

N.B. Plural as for der/die/das-words.

§7 III, IV, V — THE THREE BASIC TYPES OF ADJECTIVE ENDINGS

III Adjective endings after der/die/das and der/die/das-words (dieser, jener, jeder, welcher etc.)

	Masc.	Fem.	Neuter	Pl.
Nom.	e	e	e	en
Acc.	en	e	e	en
Gen.	en	en	en	en
Dat.	en	en	en	en

Endings are **e** or **en**: Der süße Apfel schmeckt gut.
Ich esse den süß**en** Apfel.

IV   Adjective endings after ein and ein-words (kein, mein, dein, sein, ihr, unser, etc.)

	Masc.	Fem.	Neuter	Pl.
Nom.	er	e	es	en
Acc.	en	e	es	en
Gen.	en	en	en	en
Dat.	en	en	en	en

Note: same pattern for **en** as III above.

V   Endings of adjectives 'on their own' with the noun
(i.e. with neither a der/die/das-word nor an ein-word in front)

	Masc.	Fem.	Neuter	Pl.
Nom.	er	e	es	e
Acc.	en	e	es	e
Gen.	en	er	en	er
Dat.	em	er	em	en

Endings of V are very similar to the endings of der/die/das itself, with two important exceptions:
Masculine and Neuter Genitive Singular = **en**, not **es**.

Examples of Table V Endings with Nouns

	Masc.	Fem.	Neut.	Pl.
Nom.	weißer Sand	frische Milch	rotes Fleisch	reife Bananen
Acc.	weißen Sand	frische Milch	rotes Fleisch	reife Bananen
Gen.	weißen Sandes	frischer Milch	roten Fleisches	reifer Bananen
Dat.	weißem Sand	frischer Milch	rotem Fleisch	reifen Bananen

§8 HOW TO USE THE FIVE BASIC TABLES

When putting endings on articles or adjectives three things must be checked:
(a) NUMBER — i.e. Singular or Plural
(b) GENDER — (if singular) i.e. Masculine, Feminine or Neuter
(c) CASE — i.e. Nominative, Accusative, Genitive or Dative

All the tables are shown together on the next page followed by some examples.

	Masc.	*Fem.*	*Neuter*	*Pl.*
Nom.	der	die	das	die
Acc.	den	die	das	die
Gen.	des	der	des	der
Dat.	dem	der	dem	den

I   der/die/das table

	Masc.	*Fem.*	*Neuter*	
Nom.	ein	eine	ein	
Acc.	einen	eine	ein	
Gen.	eines	einer	eines	
Dat.	einem	einer	einem	

II   ein table

	Masc.	*Fem.*	*Neuter*	*Pl.*
Nom.	e	e	e	en
Acc.	en	e	e	en
Gen.	en	en	en	en
Dat.	en	en	en	en

III   Adjective endings after der/die/das (and der/die/das-words)

	Masc.	*Fem.*	*Neuter*	*Pl.*
Nom.	er	e	es	en
Acc.	en	e	es	en
Gen.	en	en	en	en
Dat.	en	en	en	en

IV   Adjective endings after ein (and ein-words)

	Masc.	*Fem.*	*Neuter*	*Pl.*
Nom.	er	e	es	e
Acc.	en	e	es	e
Gen.	en	er	en	er
Dat.	em	er	em	en

V   Adjectives on their own with noun

Example 1   She buys *a new coat*.

What number? — singular
What gender? — masculine
What case?   — accusative

Go to table II for masculine object = accusative of **ein** = **einen**
Go to table IV for masculine object adjective ending = neu**en**

Sie kauft **einen neuen Mantel**.

Example 2   He gives it *to the old woman.*

What number? — singular
What gender? — feminine
What case?   — dative

Go to table I for singular feminine dative of **der/die/das** = **der**
Go to table III for singular feminine dative adjective ending
= alt**en**.

Er gibt es **der alten Frau.**

Example 3   *Warm clothes* are dear.

What number? — plural
What case?   — nominative

Go to table V for plural nominative adjective ending = **warme**

Warme Kleider sind teuer.

Example 4   *My old granny* is coming.

What number? — singular
What gender? — feminine
What case?   — nominative

Go to table II for singular feminine nominative of **ein** = eine,
so mein**e**
Go to table IV for singular feminine adjective ending = alt**e**

Meine alte Oma kommt.

Example 5   He says *to this little child...*

What number? — singular
What gender? — neuter
What case?   — dative

Go to table I singular neuter dative of **der/die/das** = **dem**, so
dies**em**
Go to table III singular, neuter, dative adjective ending =
klein**en**

Er sagt **diesem kleinen Kind...**

Note: (**a**) **alle** and **beide** take the adjective endings of table III:
alle gut**en** Menschen
beide jung**en** Mädchen
(**b**) viele, wenige, einige, mehrere take adjective endings of table V:
einige nett**e** Leute

§9 THE PLURAL OF *KEIN* AND THE POSSESSIVE ADJECTIVES

(**kein** = 'not a' *plural* 'no', **mein** = 'my', **dein** = 'your',
sein = 'his/its', **ihr** = 'her/its', **unser** = 'our', **euer** = 'your',
Ihr = 'your', **ihr** = 'their')

A) These **ein-words** must look elsewhere for a plural because **ein** has no plural. They take the plural endings of table V.

Nom.	e →	keine Bücher	ihre Kinder
Acc.	e →	keine Bücher	ihre Kinder
Gen.	er →	keiner Bücher	ihrer Kinder
Dat.	en →	keinen Büchern	ihren Kindern

B) If **keine** or any of the possessive adjectives in the plural are followed by an adjective, these adjectives take the plural endings of Table IV:
keine großen Bücher   seine alten Bücher

> **Note:** It is usual to drop the **e** of **eu(e)r** if it takes any ending in the singular or plural.
> eure Freundin   your friend
> mit euren Eltern   with your parents

§10 ADJECTIVES USED AFTER *ETWAS, NICHTS, VIEL, WENIG, ALLERLEI*

(i) take a capital letter plus **es** in the Nominative and Accusative:
etwas **Schönes**   something beautiful
(ii) take a capital letter plus **em** in the Dative:
mit etwas Hübsch**em**   with something pretty
Exceptions are the adjectives **andere** and **möglich which do not have capital letters:**
etwas **anderes**   nichts **mögliches**
Note: The ending after **alles** is **e:**
alles Gute!   all the best!   alles mögliche   everything possible

§11 PREDICATIVE ADJECTIVE

A predicative adjective (an adjective on its own, not in front of a noun) has no ending:
Das Wasser ist kalt.   Die Bluse ist schön.

§12 ADJECTIVAL NOUNS

Adjectival nouns are grammatically speaking still adjectives and take normal adjective endings.

ein **Alter**	an old man	eine **Alte**	an old woman
der **Alte**	the old man	die **Alte**	the old woman
die **Alten**	the old people	**Alte**	old people

Common adjectival nouns

Alte(r)	old person	Beamte(r)	official
Bekannte(r)	acquaintance	Blinde(r)	blind person
Deutsche(r)	German	Erwachsene(r)	adult
Farbige(r)	coloured person	Fremde(r)	stranger
Gefangene(r)	prisoner	Jugendliche(r)	young person
Kranke(r)	sick person	Reisende(r)	traveller
Verwandte(r)	relative	Verletzte(r)	injured person

Further examples

der Beamte (Table III)	*but* ein Beamter (Table IV)
viele Beamte	many officials (Table V)
diesen Deutschen	this German man (*acc.*, Table III)
keine Deutsche	no German woman (Table IV)
keine Deutschen	no Germans (Table IV)
Jugendliche	young people (Table V)
eines Verwandten	of a male relative (Table IV)
zum Verletzten	to the injured man (Table III)

Note the special use in the following:
wir Deutschen   we Germans   ihr Jugendlichen   you young people

Do not confuse adjectival nouns with the masculine nouns which come from verbs or place names and have the basic masculine declension of nouns:

Nom. Sing.	der Lehrer	der Berliner
Gen. Sing.	des Lehrers	des Berliners
Nom./Acc. Pl.	die Lehrer	die Berliner

Berliner and all other nouns formed from place names are also used as adjectives, in which case they do not take any ending:
die Berliner Mauer   the Berlin Wall
in der Nähe (von) der Berliner Mauer   near the Berlin Wall

§13 COMPARISON OF ADJECTIVES

A) Add **er** to the basic adjective:
klein**er**   smaller   schön**er**   more beautiful

B) If the adjective is of one syllable and can take an umlaut (i.e. the vowel is **a**, **o** or **u** then it does so:

warm → wärmer   groß → größer   klug → klüger

Among exceptions which do not umlaut are:

klar → klarer   falsch → falscher   flach → flacher   bunt → bunter
rund → runder   voll → voller
and *all* adjectives containing **au**:
braun → brauner   laut → lauter

C) **Note: immer** wärmer   warmer *and* warmer
       immer größer   bigger *and* bigger etc.

D) than = **als**:
Er ist kleiner **als** sein Bruder.   He is smaller *than* his brother.

Note also: so klein **wie, so** warm **wie**, etc. = as small, warm etc. as

§14 SUPERLATIVE OF ADJECTIVES

A) Add **st** to basic adjective.
klein**st**-   schön**st**-

If used attributively (i.e. before a noun or where a noun is understood) the superlative must have an adjective ending:
Er wohnt im schönst**en** Haus.
Das ist das kleinste (Haus).

If used predicatively or acting as an adverb, the construction is **am . . . sten** and never changes:
Der Sommer ist **am** schön**sten**. = the most beautiful (i.e. of the seasons)
Dort ist der Fluß **am** tief**sten**. = at its deepest

B) Add **est** after a basic adjective ending in **s, sch, ß, t, d.**
attributive:
der, die, das mieseste/falscheste/heißeste/lauteste/rundeste
predicative:
am miesesten/falschesten/heißesten/lautesten/rundesten

Heute ist der mieseste Tag meines Lebens.
Today is the most rotten day of my life.

Hier ist es am heißesten.
It's hottest here.

§15 IRREGULAR COMPARATIVES AND SUPERLATIVES

gut	→	besser	→	der, die, das beste am besten
viel	→	mehr	→	der, die, das meiste am meisten
groß	→	größer	→	der, die, das größte am größten

| hoch | → | höher | → | der, die, das höchste | am höchsten |
| nah | → | näher | → | der, die, das nächste | am nächsten |

Note particularly:
no **s** added in the superlative of **groß**
c omitted in the comparative of **hoch**
c inserted in the superlative of **nah**

PART THREE — PRONOUNS AND QUESTION FORMS

§16 PERSONAL PRONOUNS

A)

		I	*you*	*he/it*	*she/it*	*it*	*we*	*you*	*you*	*they*
Nom.		ich	du	er	sie	es	wir	ihr	Sie	sie
Acc.		mich	dich	ihn	sie	es	uns	euch	Sie	sie
Dat.		mir	dir	ihm	ihr	ihm	uns	euch	Ihnen	ihnen
		me	*you*	*him/it*	*her/it*	*it*	*us*	*you*	*you*	*them*

(There is a genitive of each pronoun — meiner, deiner, seiner, ihrer, unser, euer, Ihrer and ihrer — but it is rarely used.)

B) Three words for it

Whether you use **er**, **sie** or **es** depends on the gender of the noun to which 'it' refers:

    Masculine 'it' = er
    Feminine 'it' = sie
    Neuter 'it' = es

Der Apfel schmeckt gut. → **Er** schmeckt gut.
Die Rose ist schön. → **Sie** ist schön.
Das Sofa ist weich. → **Es** ist weich.

    Similarly in the accusative the word for 'it' will vary according to the gender of the noun:

    Ich kaufe **den Pulli**. → Ich kaufe **ihn**.
    Ich esse **die Banane**. → Ich esse **sie**.
    Ich nehme **das Getränk**. → Ich nehme **es**.

C) Three words for 'you'

du   ihr   Sie

The word used for 'you' depends upon whom you are addressing and whether the situation is familiar or formal:

(i) Speaking to one child, animal, member of the family or friend:
    use **du**

(ii) Speaking to more than one child, animal, member of the family or friend:
    use **ihr**

(iii) Speaking to one *or more* persons not in the above groups (i.e. mainly people you don't know or don't know well):
    use **Sie** (singular *and* plural)

Distinguishing the use of these words may be helped by the use of the

mnemonic (aid to memory) CAFF (= Child, Animal, Friend, Family)
One CAFF — — — — — — — — — —use **du** for 'you'.
Two or more CAFFs — — — — —use **ihr** for 'you'
Non-CAFF or CAFFs — — — — —use **Sie** for 'you'
   Mein Kind, wohin gehst **du?**
   Kinder, wohin geht **ihr?**
   Herr Braun, wohin gehen **Sie?**
   Meine Herren, wohin gehen **Sie?**
The CAFF rule applies to 'your' as
well as 'you':
du for 'you' — — — — — — — — —**dein** = your
ihr for 'you' — — — — — — — — —**euer** = your
Sie for 'you' — — — — — — — — —**Ihr** = your
   Du sagst, daß er **dein** Freund ist.
   Ihr sagt, daß er **euer** Freund ist.
   Sie sagen, daß er **Ihr** Freund ist.

§17 POSSESSIVE PRONOUNS

A)

meiner	—	mine
deiner	—	yours
seiner	—	his
ihrer	—	hers
unserer	—	ours
eurer	—	yours
Ihrer	—	yours
ihrer	—	theirs

CAFF also applies here

B) Declension

	Masc.	*Fem.*	*Neut.*	*Pl.*
Nom.	meiner	meine	mein(e)s	meine
Acc.	meinen	meine	mein(e)s	meine
Gen.	meines	meiner	meines	meiner
Dat.	meinem	meiner	meinem	meinen

C) Gender, number and case

(i) The gender (whether masculine, feminine or neuter) of the possessive pronoun is the gender of the noun to which it refers.
   Wo ist **dein** Buch (*neuter*)? — **Mein(e)s** ist hier.

(ii) The number (singular or plural) of the possessive pronoun is the number of the noun to which it refers:
   Wo sind **deine** Kleider? — **Meine** sind hier.

(iii) The possessive pronoun has its own case, depending on its use in the sentence.
   Wo ist **dein** Salat (*nominative*)? — Ich habe **meinen**. (*accusative*)

Dein Wagen (*nominative*) sieht sehr schön aus — mit **meinem** (*dative*) nicht zu vergleichen!
Your car looks very nice — not to be compared with mine!

§18 The pronoun *man*

man can only be the *subject* of the verb:
   In der Zeitung liest **man** ...   In the newspaper one reads ...
Accusative is **einen**:
   Seine Faulheit ärgert **einen**.   His laziness annoys one.
Dative is **einem**:
   Er hilft **einem**, wenn er kann.   He helps one, if he can. (helfen + *dative*)
Note: Do not confuse the noun **der Mann** with the pronoun **man**.

§19 *Wer?* — Who?

wer declines:

Nom.	wer?	who?
Acc.	wen?	whom?
Gen.	wessen?	whose?
Dat.	wem?	to whom?

Wer ist da?	Who is there?
Wen kennst du hier?	Whom do you know here?
Wessen Auto ist das?	Whose car is that?
Wem schenkt er die Blumen?	To whom is he giving the flowers?

§20 There is/There are

es ist	=	there is	+ *nominative case*
es sind	=	there are	+ *nominative case*
es war	=	there was	+ *nominative case*
es waren	=	there were	+ *nominative case*

es gibt	=	there is *or* there are + *accusative case*
es gab	=	there was *or* there were + *accusative case*

Which to use — es ist or es gibt?

es ist, es sind etc. — more specific **Es ist** ein Stuhl da!
es gibt etc. — more general   **Es gibt** viele Menschen auf der Welt.
   There are (= there exist) many people in the world.
or describing an event:
   Es gab ein Gewitter.   There was a thunderstorm.

Sometimes either is possible, **es ist/sind** being less formal:
  Es sind/gibt viele Äpfel auf dem Baum.
  There are a lot of apples on the tree.
Note also: das sind = those are:
  Das sind meine Klamotten.   Those are my things (belongings).

§21 THE RELATIVE PRONOUN — WHO, WHICH, THAT (WHICH)

A)

	Masc.	*Fem.*	*Neuter*	*Pl.*
Nom.	der	die	das	die
Acc.	den	die	das	die
Gen.	dessen	deren	dessen	deren
Dat.	dem	der	dem	denen

The relative pronoun declines like the definite article with the following exceptions:
  Gen. masc. & neuter   **dessen**
  Gen. fem. & pl.   **deren**
  Dat. pl.   **denen**

B) Whose — 'dessen' or 'deren'?

The gender/number must be the gender/number of the noun to which it refers. ←
  Der Mann, **dessen** Frau . . .   The man whose wife . . .
  Die Frau, **deren** Mann . . .   The wife, whose husband . . .
  Die Eltern, **deren** Sohn . . .   The parents whose son . . .

C) Which, that (masculine) — 'der' or 'den'?

Example 1: The ballpen, that I bought yesterday, was quite cheap.

(i) Imagine a box round the clause introduced by 'that':

> that I bought yesterday

(ii) Look for the subject — in this case 'I'

(iii) So 'that' (or 'which') must be the object = **den**:
  Der Kugelschreiber, **den** ich gestern gekauft habe, war ganz billig.

Example 2: The cake which tastes best is on the table.

(i) Imagine a box round the clause introduced by 'which':

> which tastes best

(ii) Look for the subject in the box; it must be 'which'
(no other possibility)

(iii) So translate 'which' by nominative **der**:
Der Kuchen, **der** am besten schmeckt, ist auf dem Tisch.

§22 RELATIVE PRONOUN *WAS*

Was is used in German when referring to the whole of the previous clause, not simply to one noun in the clause, i.e. meaning 'a fact which'

Er bestand das Examen, **was** mir viel Freude macht.
He passed the exam, (a fact) which pleases me a lot.

Notice the use of **was** in the following:

das, was	—	that which, what
alles, was	—	all/everything that
nichts, was	—	nothing that
wenig or weniges, was	—	little that
viel or vieles, was	—	much that
das Beste, was	—	the best that

e.g. Er hörte alles, was ich sagte.
He heard all that I said.

In the phrase **das, was** the **das** is often omitted:
Was mich am meisten stört, ist . . .   What worries me most is . . .

§23 QUESTION FORMS

wann?	when?	**wogegen?**	against what?
warum?	why?	**wohinter?**	behind what?
weshalb?	for what reason?	**womit?**	with what?
was?	what?	**wonach?**	after what?
was für (ein)?	what kind of (a)?	**woran?**	on what? by what?
welcher?	which/which one?	**worauf?**	on what?
wer?	who?	**woraus?**	out of what?
wessen?	whose?	**worin?**	in what?
wieviel?	how much?	**worüber?**	over what?
wie viele?	how many?	**worum?**	around what?
wo?	where?	**worunter?**	under what?
woher?	where from?	**wovon?**	from what?
wohin?	where to?	**wovor?**	in front of what?
wodurch?	through where?	**wozu?**	to what/to what
wofür?	for what?		purpose/why?

Finally note the following uses of pronouns:
einer (*masc.*) der Jungen = one of the boys
kein(e)s (*neuter*) der Mädchen = none of the girls
(**einer** and **keiner** decline like the possessive pronouns — see Section 17b)

Jeder kann es.   Anyone can do it.
Er selbst hat das Flugzeug gebastelt.   He put the plane together himself.

Er ist nicht irgend jemand.   He is not just anyone.
Das ist der, der die Drogen eingeschmuggelt hat.   That's the one who
smuggled in the drugs.

Sie sagt immer dasselbe.   She always says the same thing.

Ich bin es!   It's me!

PART FOUR — VERB FORMS AND TYPES

§24 INFINITIVE

A) **Meaning** to do something

B) **Formation** verb stem + infinitive ending **en** or **n**
   lach|en   lächel|n   wander|n   tu|n

§25 PRESENT TENSE

A) **Meaning** ich kaufe = I buy/I do buy/I am buying

B) **Formation** verb stem + present tense endings

kaufen to buy		lächeln to smile		wandern to hike, roam	
ich	kauf **e**	ich	lächl **e**	ich	wander **e**
du	kauf **st**	du	lächl **st**	du	wander **st**
er/sie/es	kauf **t**	er/sie/es	lächl **t**	er/sie/es	wander **t**
wir	kauf **en**	wir	lächl **n**	wir	wander **n**
ihr	kauf **t**	ihr	lächl **t**	ihr	wander **t**
Sie	kauf **en**	Sie	lächl **n**	Sie	wander **n**
sie	kauf **en**	sie	lächl **n**	sie	wander **n**

The **wir/Sie/sie**-forms, apart from those of **sein**, are always the same as the infinitive.
*In the **du**-form, where the stem ends in **s** or an **s** sound, the **es** drops out:
   fassen → du fassest → du **faßt**
   sitzen → du sitzest → du **sitzt**

C) If the stem of the verb ends in **d**, **t**, **m** or **n**, an **e** is inserted between stem and ending except where there is one already to assist pronunciation:

ich rede		ich arbeite		ich atme		ich trockne	
du red	**est**	du arbeit	**est**	du atm	**est**	du trockn	**est**
	et		**et**		**et**		**et**
	en		**en**		**en**		**en**
	et		**et**		**et**		**et**
	en		**en**		**en**		**en**
	en		**en**		**en**		**en**

D) Note: Remember in all tenses the importance of subject and verb agreement.

Singular Subject   —   *Singular* Verb
Plural Subject   —   *Plural* Verb
Der Mann wacht auf.   The man wakes up.
Die Männer wachen auf.   The men wake up.
Der Mann und die Frau gehen nach Hause.   The man and woman go home.

E) Irregular Present Tense
To make life easier remember there is only one verb in German which is irregular in the plural:
sein to be

ich bin	wir sind
du bist	ihr seid
er/sie/es ist	Sie sind
	sie sind

F) Most irregular present tenses are irregular only in the **du-** and **er/sie/es**-forms; e.g. **schlafen** (to sleep) which takes an umlaut in the **du-** and **er/sie/es**-forms only:

ich schlafe	wir schlafen
du schläfst	ihr schlaft
er/sie/es schläft	Sie schlafen
	sie schlafen

Examples of other verbs like **schlafen** taking an umlaut are: —
fahren — to drive, travel   fallen — to fall
laufen — to run   lassen — to let, leave
*Remember also stem ending in **s** (see Section 25b) hence **du läßt**.

G) Other verbs change the vowel in **du-** and **er**-forms: **e → ie**.

ich sehe → du siehst — er sieht
ich stehle → du stiehlst — er stiehlt
ich lese → du liest — er liest

H) Some verbs change the vowel **e → i**:

ich breche → du brichst — er bricht
ich esse → du ißt — er ißt
ich gebe → du gibst — er gibt
ich vergesse → du vergißt — er vergißt
ich werfe → du wirfst — er wirft

I) Note the spelling of the following especially:

braten	(to roast, fry)	du brätst — er brät
haben	(to have)	du hast — er hat
halten	(to stop, halt)	du hältst — er hält

einladen	(to invite)	du lädst ein — er lädt ein
nehmen	(to take)	du nimmst — er nimmt
raten	(to advise)	du rätst — er rät
treten	(to step)	du trittst — er tritt
werden	(to become)	du wirst — er wird

J) Some important German verbs (chiefly the so-called modal verbs, see Section 42) are also irregular in the **ich**-form, i.e. wissen (to know) and modal verbs können, wollen, müssen, dürfen, mögen and sollen.

wissen *to know*	**können** *to be able to*	**wollen** *to wish, want to*
ich weiß ← ⌐ du weißt │ er/sie/es weiß ← ┘	ich kann ← ⌐ du kannst │ er/sie/es kann ← ┘	ich will ← ⌐ du willst │ er/sie/es will ← ┘
müssen *to have to, must*	**mögen** *to like to, to like*	**sollen** *am to, ought to*
ich muß ← ⌐ du mußt │ er/sie/es muß ← ┘	ich mag ← ⌐ du magst │ er/sie/es mag ← ┘	ich soll ← ⌐ du sollst │ er/sie/es soll ← ┘

Irregular Present Tenses will be found either in the verb table (Section 49) or in a dictionary.

§26 IMPERFECT TENSE

A) Meaning ich lachte = I laughed/I did laugh/I used to laugh/I was
laughing

B) Formation: In German as in English there are two ways of forming the Imperfect Tense.

(i) The Regular or Weak Verb (English ed = German **te**)

ich lach **te**	wir lach **ten**	
du lach **test**	ihr lach **tet**	
er/sie/es lach **te**	Sie lach **ten**	
	sie lach **ten**	

If the stem ends in **d, t, m** or **n** add the extra **e** throughout:
    ich red**ete**   ich arbeit**ete**   ich atm**ete**   ich trockn**ete**

(ii) The Irregular or Strong Verb

Formation: In German as in English by vowel change in the stem:
   English I sing →I sang   *German* ich **singe** → ich **sang**
          I come →I came   ich **komme**→ ich **kam**
          I fly   →I flew   ich **fliege** → ich **flog**

ich flog NO ENDING	wir flog **en**
du flog **st**	ihr flog **t**
er/sie/es flog NO ENDING	Sie flog **en**
	sie flog **en**

C) **Mixed Verbs** are so called because they are a mixture of (i) and (ii) above. They are regular because they take the **-te**, **-test**, **-te** endings of the regular imperfect. They are irregular because they change the stem vowel.

brennen	→	brannte
bringen	→	brachte
denken	→	dachte
kennen	→	kannte
nennen	→	nannte
rennen	→	rannte
wissen	→	wußte

D) The big question is whether the verb is regular or irregular (weak or strong). If in doubt look in the Verb Table (Section 49) or in a dictionary. If the verb is not in the tables, then the verb is regular.

E) Remember when looking up a verb in the Verb Table (Section 49) to remove any prefix first. For example, **nehmen** has the following possible prefixes: **an-, ab-, auf-, be-, durch-, ein-, entgegen-, fort-, her-, heraus-, hin-, teil-, über-, ver-, vor-, weg-, zu-, zurück-,** and **zusammen-** to mention only the most common!

§27 FUTURE TENSE

A) **Meaning:** ich werde/er wird zahlen = I shall/he will pay

B) **Formation:** Present Tense of **werden** + infinitive of the verb concerned.

ich	werde	zahlen
du	wirst	zahlen
er/sie/es	wird	zahlen
wir	werden	zahlen
ihr	werdet	zahlen
Sie	werden	zahlen
sie	werden	zahlen

Note 1: The infinitive in German always goes to the end of the clause or sentence:
Ich werde morgen zahlen.

Note 2: The future is often translated in German by the Present Tense:
Er kommt nächste Woche.

Note 3: Do not confuse **ich will** and **ich werde**:
Ich will zahlen.   = I want to pay.
Ich werde zahlen. = I shall pay.

§28 CONDITIONAL TENSE

A) Meaning: ich würde zahlen = I would pay

B) Formation: würde + infinitive

ich	würde zahlen	wir	würden zahlen
du	würdest zahlen	ihr	würdet zahlen
er/sie/es	würde zahlen	Sie	würden zahlen
		sie	würden zahlen

§29 PERFECT TENSE

A) Meaning: Ich habe gelacht. = I have laughed./I have been laughing./
I laughed.
Ich bin gelaufen. = I have run./I have been running./I ran.

B) Formation: Present Tense of **haben** *or* **sein** + past participle.

ich	habe		ich	bin	
du	hast		du	bist	
er/sie/es	hat		er/sie/es	ist	
wir	haben	gelacht	wir	sind	gelaufen
ihr	habt		ihr	seid	
Sie	haben		Sie	sind	
sie	haben		sie	sind	

C) Whether to use **haben** or **sein**? Most verbs take **haben**. Nearly all the verbs taking **sein** are strong verbs and are shown as taking **sein** in the verb table (Section 49) or in a better German dictionary.

D) Examples of verbs taking 'sein'

   (i) Verbs of motion, e.g. eintreffen (to arrive), gehen, kommen, landen, rennen, rutschen (to slip), wandern (to roam)

   (ii) Changes of state, e.g. aufwachen (to wake up), einschlafen (to fall asleep), frieren (to freeze), sterben (to die)

   (iii) Verbs with a dative object e.g. begegnen (to meet (by chance)), folgen (to follow)

   (iv) sein (to be), werden (to become), bleiben (to remain), geschehen (to happen), passieren (to happen), verschwinden (to disappear)

E) Note: Remember a verb normally taking **sein** will take **haben** if the verb has a direct object:

> Ich habe den Wagen zu schnell gefahren.
> I have driven the car too fast.

F) Formation of the Past Participle

(i) **Regular Weak Past Participle** e.g. of lachen
   Formation: *a)* Take the stem   → **lach**
   b) Put **ge** in front   → **gelach**
   c) Put **t** at the end   → **gelacht**
   Again note the extra **e** in
   geredet   gearbeitet   geatmet   getrocknet

(ii) **Irregular Strong Past Participle.** You must look it up in the verb table or a dictionary.

(iii) **Past Participle of verbs with Inseparable Prefixes**
   The following prefixes
   be- ge- emp- ent- er- ver- zer- miß- do not separate from the verb and have no **ge** in the past participle:
   e.g. bedecken   Past Participle   bedeckt
   entdecken   entdeckt

(iv) **Past Participles of Foreign Based Verbs ending in -ieren**
   These verbs also have no **ge** in the Past Participle:
   e.g. fotografieren   Past Participle   fotografiert
   telefonieren   telefoniert
   However note the irregular verb verlieren, p.p. verloren

(v) **Past Participles of Verbs with Separable Prefixes**
   The **ge** of the past participle is inserted between the prefix and the verb stem:
   e.g. herunterholen   →   herunter**ge**holt
   abgehen   →   ab**ge**gangen

(vi) **Prefixes sometimes separable, sometimes inseparable**
   Particularly, **durch-, über-, um-.** Here are three senses of durchfahren:
   1) durchfahren (*separable*) = to drive/travel straight through (without stopping)
      Er ist bei Rot durchgefahren.   He went through (the lights) on red.
   2) durchfahren (*inseparable*) = to drive through (*with direct object*)
      Wir haben den Schwarzwald durchfahren.   We drove through the Black Forest.
   3) durchfahren (*inseparable*) = to go through (*in an abstract sense*)
      Der Gedanke hat ihn durchfahren.   The thought has struck him.
   Any decent dictionary will show when and with which meaning these prefixes are separable or inseparable.
   Note that a) a verb with an inseparable prefix is always transitive; b) in speech, with inseparable verbs, the stress is on the verb, not on the prefix.

G) Summary by examples of perfect tense

Ich habe gelacht.	(basic weak past participle)
Ich habe geredet.	(extra 'e' in past participle)
Ich habe geöffnet.	(extra 'e')
Ich habe geantwortet.	(extra 'e')
Ich habe bedeckt.	(inseparable prefix — no **ge**)
Ich habe heruntergeholt.	(**ge** after separable prefix)
Ich habe telefoniert.	(foreign word, no **ge**)
Wir haben gesungen.	(strong verb with **haben**)
Wir sind gelaufen.	(strong verb with **sein**)
Ich bin aufgestanden.	(strong verb with **sein** and separable prefix)
Ich habe versprochen.	(strong verb with inseparable prefix)
Wir sind ihm gefolgt.	(weak verb with **sein**)

Note: the Past Participle, like the infinitive, goes to the end of the clause or sentence:

Sie hat das Kleid **gekauft**.   She has bought the dress.

§30 PERFECT OR IMPERFECT TENSE TO EXPRESS, FOR EXAMPLE 'I LAUGHED'?

The two tenses are frequently interchangeable. A general guideline is that in familiar, colloquial speech or letter writing the perfect tense would be preferred. In more formal situations and for literary style, one would expect to find the imperfect.

§31 PLUPERFECT TENSE

A) Meaning: Ich hatte geweint. = I had cried./I had been crying.
Er war gelaufen. = He had run./He had been running.

B) Formation: Imperfect of **haben** or **sein** + past participle.

ich	hatte		ich	war	
du	hattest		du	warst	
er/sie/es	hatte		er/sie/es	war	
wir	hatten	geweint	wir	waren	gelaufen
ihr	hattet		ihr	wart	
Sie	hatten		Sie	waren	
sie	hatten		sie	waren	

§32 FUTURE PERFECT

A) Meaning: Er wird es gelernt haben = he will have learnt it./He has probably learnt it.
Er wird gelaufen sein = He will have run./He has probably run.

B) Formation: $\frac{1}{2}$ Future Tense and $\frac{1}{2}$ Perfect Tense, i.e. present of **werden** + past participle + infinitive of **haben** or **sein**:

Er wird geweint haben.	Er wird gekommen sein.
Sie werden geweint haben.	Sie werden gekommen sein.

§33 REFLEXIVE VERBS

A) Meanings:

(i) Expressing the idea of doing something to oneself:
sich waschen = to wash (oneself).

(ii) Conveying the idea of interaction:
Wir kennen uns. = We know one another.

(iii) Expressing independent action:
Die Tür öffnet sich. = The door opens.

B) Formation: The German reflexive pronoun, like the English one, comes after the verb, except in the infinitive:

sich waschen, to wash			
ich	wasche mich	wir	waschen uns
du	wäschst dich	ihr	ihr wascht euch
er/sie/es	wäschst sich	Sie	Sie waschen sich
		sie	sie waschen sich

Note: the reflexive pronoun is the same as the personal pronoun, except for the 3rd person (always **sich**)

C) Dative Reflexive

(i) With parts of the body as object the dative of the reflexive pronoun is used rather than the possessive adjective:
Du wäschst **dir** das Gesicht.   You wash your face.
Note the difference in meaning of the following:
Er kämmt **sich** das Haar. = He combs his (own) hair.
Er kämmt **ihm** das Haar.   = He combs his (= someone else's) hair.
Remember:
sich is the one case where the reflexive pronoun is different from the personal pronoun
sich is both dative *and* accusative, singular *and* plural

(ii) sich etwas machen lassen — to have something done
Ich ließ **mir** ein Rezept verschreiben.   I had a prescription made
out.

§34 IMPERATIVE (COMMAND)

A) Decide which 'you' is required:

1 CAFF	= du
2 or more CAFFS	= ihr
NON CAFF/NON CAFFS	= Sie

B) Regular Command Endings

mach(e)   — to someone you would call **du**
macht   — to people you would address as **ihr**
machen Sie — to a person or persons addressed as **Sie**
So only the **du** form is different from the present tense.

C) With reflexive:

schnalle dich an! ⎫
schnallt euch an! ⎬   Fasten your seat belt(s)
schnallen Sie sich an! ⎭

D) Note 1: **e** ending of the 1 CAFF or du form is often dropped leaving
the stem only:
mach schnell!   get a move on!

Note 2: The words **doch, mal, schon** are often put with the imperative
of the verb to lend further emphasis, although mal and schon
have little or no effect on the sense:

Mach doch schnell!	*Do* be quick!
Singen Sie doch!	*Go on*, sing!
Seid doch nicht so blöde!	*Don't* be so silly!
Sag mal, was du da hast!	Tell me what you've got there!
Komm schon!	Come along!

E) Irregular Command Forms

There is only one verb which has more than one irregular command
form: **sein**.

Sei ruhig!	1 CAFF	⎫	
Seid ruhig!	2 or more CAFFS	⎬	Be quiet!
Seien Sie ruhig!	NON CAFF(S)	⎭	

F) Other irregular command forms only occur:

(i) In the 1 CAFF or **du** form

(ii) When the strong verb changes the vowel of its stem in the singular of
the present tense e.g.

PRESENT			IMPERATIVE		
Irregular			Irregular	Regular	Regular
geben	to give	gibt	gib	gebt	geben Sie
lesen	to read	liest	lies	lest	lesen Sie
nehmen	to take	nimmt	nimm	nehmt	nehmen Sie
sehen	to see	sieht	sieh(e)	seht	sehen Sie
sprechen	to speak	spricht	sprich	sprecht	sprechen Sie
vergessen	to forget	vergißt	vergiß	vergeßt	vergessen Sie

G) Translating 'let us (do something)'

Turn round the **wir**-form of the present tense:
Singen wir!   Let us sing!

H) Infinitive for Command (Instructions)

The infinitive is often used for instructions in official notices, directions and recipes:
Aufpassen!   Watch out! Pay attention!
Hunde an der Leine halten.   Keep dogs on a lead.
Nicht hinauslehnen.   Don't lean out.
Nicht rauchen.   Do not smoke.
Filmpatrone in die Filmkammer einlegen.   Place the film cartridge in the film chamber.
Etwas Pfeffer hinzugeben.   Add some pepper.

§35 THE PASSIVE TENSES

A) Meaning: The subject has something done to it:

Der Fußboden wird gebohnert.   The floor is being polished.
Die Juwelen wurden gestohlen.   The jewels were stolen.

B) Basic Form of the Passive: part of **werden** + past participle

C) The Tenses in the Passive

Present Passive
Construction — Present Tense of **werden** + past participle
Der Kuchen wird gegessen.   The cake is eaten.

Imperfect Passive
Construction — Imperfect of **werden** + past participle.
Der Kuchen wurde gegessen.   The cake was eaten.

Future Passive
Construction — Present of **werden** + past participle + **werden**
.(infinitive)
Der Kuchen wird gegessen werden.   The cake will be eaten.

Conditional Passive
Construction — **würde** etc. + past participle + **werden** (infinitive)
   Der Kuchen würde gegessen werden.   The cake would be eaten.

Perfect Passive
Construction — Present of **sein** + past participle + **worden**
   Der Kuchen ist gegessen worden.   The cake has been eaten.

Pluperfect Passive
Construction — Imperfect of **sein** + past participle + **worden**
   Der Kuchen war gegessen worden.   The cake had been eaten.

D) The word for 'by' with the Passive

General Guideline
   'by' + person or animal → **von** + dative:
      Der Kuchen wurde von einem Kind gegessen.
      The cake was eaten by a child.
      Er wurde von einem Hund gebissen.
      He was bitten by a dog.

   'by' + inanimate object with sense of 'through' → **durch** + accusative:
      Sein Leben wurde durch eine Transfusion gerettet.
      His life was saved by (= through) a blood transfusion.

E) Passive of Verbs + Dative

Verbs + dative cannot be literally turned into the passive.
The impersonal **es** form must be used:
   Es wurde ihm geholfen.
   He was helped. (i.e. 'It was helped to him')
The **es** can be omitted: Ihm wurde geholfen.

§36 USE OF PASSIVE

A) The Passive is used:

  (i) To indicate the action is, or was going on at a particular time:
      Das Haus wird gebaut.
      The house is being built.
      Das Haus wurde im Jahre 1982 gebaut.
      The house was built in 1982.

  (ii) To indicate an occurrence
      Er wurde von seinen Eltern bestraft.
      He was punished by his parents.

B) The Passive is *not* used if one is describing a completed state. Instead the past participle is used as an adjective with **sein**:

   Das Haus ist solide gebaut.
   The house is solidly built.
   Er war erschöpft.
   He was exhausted.

§37 ALTERNATIVES TO THE PASSIVE

German avoids the passive more than English, especially if cumbersome.

A) By turning the sentence round:

> Der Dieb ist von der Polizei gefaßt worden.
> becomes
> Die Polizei hat den Dieb gefaßt.
> The police caught the thief.

B) By using **man** = 'one':

> Der Kuchen war gegessen worden.
> becomes
> Man hatte den Kuchen gegessen.
> literally: 'One had eaten the cake.'

Note also the simple alternative: man half ihm = 'one helped him', for the passive of a verb + dative (Section 35(e))

Note: Do not confuse the Future Active Tense with Passive Tenses.
> Future Tense = **werden** + INFINITIVE
> Passive Tense = **werden** + PAST PARTICIPLE
> e.g. ich werde alles kaufen.   I shall buy everything.
> ich werde immer gesehen.   I am always seen.

§38 THE SUBJUNCTIVE MOOD

A) **Present Subjunctive**

Formation: stem of infinitive + **e, est, e, en, et, en, en**
(Note **e** in each ending)
e.g. **wissen:**

ich wiss **e**	wir wiss **en**
du wiss **est**	ihr wiss **et**
er/sie/es wiss **e**	Sie wiss **en**
	sie wiss **en**

This formation is the same for all verbs, both regular and irregular.
In the case of regular verbs it is the same as the ordinary present apart from 2nd and 3rd person singular:
> 2nd is always **-est**
> 3rd is always **-e** instead of **-t**
> Hence haben → du habest   er habe
> werden → du werdest   er werde

The ONLY irregular Present Subjunctive is **sein** and it is irregular only in the singular:

ich **sei**   du **seist**   er **sei**

The plural is regular:

wir seien   ihr seiet   Sie seien   sie seien

B) Imperfect Subjunctive

2 Types of Imperfect Subjunctive

(i) Imperfect Subjunctive of Regular Weak Verbs

The Imperfect Subjunctive of the regular weak verb is the same form as the ordinary Imperfect (Imperfect Indicative):

e.g. kaufte = Imperfect Indicative AND Imperfect Subjunctive

(ii) Imperfect Subjunctive of Irregular Strong Verbs

1) Take the Imperfect Indicative Stem

war   hatt   wurd   kam   ging

2) Add Umlaut if possible

wär   hätt   würd   käm   ging (ging cannot take an umlaut)

3) Add the same endings as for Present Subjunctive:

wäre	hätte	würde	käme	ginge
wärest	hättest	würdest	kämest	gingest
wäre	hätte	würde	käme	ginge
wären	hätten	würden	kämen	gingen
wäret	hättet	würdet	kämet	ginget
wären	hätten	würden	kämen	gingen
wären	hätten	würden	kämen	gingen

Note: *the following irregular Imperfect Subjunctives:*

	helfen	→	hülfe
	sterben	→	stürbe
	werfen	→	würfe
	brennen	→	brennte
	nennen	→	nennte
	rennen	→	rennte
but	bringen	→	brächte
	denken	→	dächte

Note also the Imperfect Subjunctive of Modal Verbs:

	müssen	→	müßte
	dürfen	→	dürfte
	können	→	könnte
	mögen	→	möchte

but wollen and sollen *never* take an umlaut:

wollte/sollte = Imperfect indicative and subjunctive.

C) Future Subjunctive

Formation: Present Subjunctive of **werden** + infinitive (therefore the same as the ordinary future except for the 2nd and 3rd person singular)

e.g. Er meinte, du **werdest**/er **werde gewinnen.**

He thought you/he might win it.

D) Perfect Subjunctive

Formation: Present Subjunctive of **haben** or **sein** + past participle
  e.g. Er sagte, er **habe es gekauft.**
  Ich sagte, ich **sei gefallen.**

E) Pluperfect Subjunctive

Formation: Imperfect Subjunctive of **haben** or **sein** + past participle
  e.g. Er **hätte es gekauft**, wenn es billiger **gewesen wäre.**

§39 Major Uses of the Subjunctive

A)
(i) In indirect speech, question, belief, writing, thinking, dreaming etc.,
  introduced *by the past tense(s).*
    Er sagte, sie **sei** hier.
    Er fragte, ob sie hier **sei.**
    Er glaubte, daß sie hier **sei.**
    Er schrieb, daß sie hier **sei.**
    Er dachte, daß sie hier **sei.**
    Er träumte, daß sie hier **sei.**
  (*Present* Subjunctive used because the tense of the subjunctive depends
  on what was originally said, i.e. "Sie **ist** hier." She IS here)

(ii) If the subjunctive is used in indirect speech, belief etc. after the
  present tense, doubt or suspicion of the truth of the statement is
  implied:
    e.g. Er meint, er **verstehe** alles.
    He *thinks* he understands everything. (but does he?)

B) In Conditional Sentences Stages 2 and 3.
  There are 3 Stages of conditional sentence:

  Stage 1 I shall see him if he comes.
  Stage 2 I would see him if he came.
  Stage 3 I would have seen him if he had come.

  Stage 1 Ich **werde** ihn **sehen**, wenn er **kommt.** (No subjunctive)
  Stage 2 Construction: Main clause-Conditional Tense, Conditional
       clause-Imperfect Subjunctive
       Ich **würde** ihn **sehen**, wenn er **käme.**
       (The Conditional Tense itself is formed by the Imperfect
       Subjunctive of **werden**, i.e. **würde** + infinitive — see §28)
  Stage 3 Construction: Pluperfect Subjunctive in each section
       Ich **hätte** ihn **gesehen**, wenn er **gekommen wäre.**

§40 SHORTER SUBJUNCTIVE VERSION OF THE CONDITIONAL TENSE

Imperfect Subjunctive can be used instead of the Conditional Tense, *with a strong verb only*:

    e.g. Ich **würde laufen.**   →   Ich **liefe.**
          Ich **würde fahren.**   →   Ich **führe.**

hätte and **wäre** (see stage 3) are already such shorter forms.

  Specially useful constructions are:

  ich **möchte gern**   ⎫
  ich **hätte gern**   ⎬   I should like
               ⎭

N.B. Some of the irregular Imperfect Subjunctives are rare or dated, such as **hülfe** from **helfen** and **stürbe** from **sterben**. If in doubt use the form with **würde** — but never as a substitute for **hätte, wäre** or **möchte**.

§41 THE MANY USES OF *WERDEN*

A) **Werden** is a verb in its own right meaning 'to become':

    e.g. Er wird alt.   Sie ist krank geworden.
          Es wurde spät.   Er war Millionär geworden.

B) **But is also used to form the following** *tenses*:

Future	—	er **wird** kaufen
Conditional	—	er **würde** kaufen
Future Perfect	—	er **wird** gekauft **haben**
Passive Tenses;		
Present Passive	—	er **wird** gesehen
Imperfect Passive	—	er **wurde** gesehen
Future Passive	—	er **wird** gesehen **werden**
Conditional Passive	—	er **würde** gesehen **werden**
Perfect Passive	—	er **ist** gesehen **worden**
Pluperfect Passive	—	er **war** gesehen **worden**
Conditional Perfect Passive	—	er **wäre** gesehen **worden** (= he would have been seen)

§42 MODAL VERBS

A) Meanings:

dürfen = (i) to be allowed to; (ii) (imperf. subj.) should

(i) Darf ich mitkommen?   May I come?
(ii) Er dürfte jetzt dort sein.   He should be there by now.

dürfen nicht = (i) not to be allowed to, must not; (ii) (imperf. subj.) should not

(i) Ich darf nicht mitkommen.   I am not allowed to come.
Er darf es nicht wissen.   He must not know about it.
(ii) Er dürfte nicht rauchen.   He shouldn't smoke.
Note: dürfte = 'should' is imperfect subjunctive;
durfte (imperfect indicative) = 'was allowed to':
Er durfte Radio hören.   He was allowed to listen to the radio.

können = to be able, can

Er kann schwimmen.
Sometimes the infinitive is understood after modal verbs
Ich kann Deutsch.   I can speak German.
Sie kann nicht mehr.   She can do no more *or* go no
                          further.

mögen = **(i)** to like; **(ii)** may

(i) Ich mag Pralinen essen.   I like to eat chocolates.
Ich mag Pralinen.   I like chocolates.
(ii) Das mag wohl sein.   That may well be true.

müssen = must, have to
Er muß heute kommen.   He must come today.
Er muß ins Bett (gehen).   He has to go to bed.
N.B. Note the difference between
Er muß nicht heute kommen   He doesn't have to come today
and
Er darf nicht heute kommen.   He must not come today.

sollen = **(i)** must; (*past*) should, ought to; **(ii)** be supposed to, be said to

(i) Er soll gleich kommen.   He must come right now.
Expression of a command (*Present Tense*)
Du solltest das schon wissen.   You should know that already.
Indication of what is fitting, sensible (*Past Tense*)
(ii) Er soll/sollte morgen kommen.   He is/was supposed to come
tomorrow.
Er soll krank sein. He is said to be ill.

wollen = **(i)** to want to; **(ii)** to be about to/on the point of.

(i) Er will ins Kino gehen.   He wants to go to the cinema.
Er will in die Stadt (gehen).   He wants to go to town.
(ii) Er wollte (eben) abfahren.   He was (just) about to go.

B) Note: A literal translation of the following is not possible because the
subject changes:

He wants *me* to come. = Er will, **daß** ich komme.
He would like *me* to do it. = Er möchte, **daß** ich es tue.

C) Note: Do not use **zu** before an infinitive dependent on a modal verb:

Er will jetzt schlafen. (*no* **zu**)
Er muß essen. (*no* **zu**)

D) Modal Verbs and Their Past Participles

Modal verbs have past participles (gedurft, gekonnt, gemocht, gemußt, gesollt, gewollt), but they are only used where there is a direct object and no infinitive:

Ich habe es gekonnt.	I have been able to (do it).
Ich habe es gemußt.	I have had to (do it).

If, however, as nearly always happens, the modal verb is used in the Perfect, Pluperfect or Conditional Perfect with the infinitive of another verb, the infinitive of the modal verb is used instead of the past participle:

Ich habe kommen **müssen**.	I have had to come.
Ich hatte es immer kaufen **wollen**.	I had always wanted to buy it.
Er hätte es finden **sollen**.	He ought to have found it.

    Note: The *modal* infinitive comes last.

§43 USE OF INFINITIVE INSTEAD OF PAST PARTICIPLE

This also applies to **sehen**, **hören** and **lassen** when they occur with another verb. These verbs also come last.

Ich habe ihn kommen **sehen**.	I have seen him coming.
Ich habe ihn kommen **hören**.	I have heard him coming.
Ich habe ihn kommen **lassen**.	I have let him come.

§44 LASSEN

Meanings:

A) to leave something somewhere:

    Ich habe meine Brille zuhause gelassen.
    I have left my glasses at home.

B) to let, allow:

    Laß ihn gehen!   Let him go!
    Note here **fallenlassen**, to let fall, i.e. drop:
    Er hat seine Uhr fallenlassen.
    He has dropped his watch.

C) to have something done:

> Er ließ sich ein Haus bauen.
> He had a house built.
> Sie läßt sich das Haar schneiden.
> She is having her hair cut.
> Mutti läßt den Arzt kommen.
> Mother is sending for the doctor.

D) to stop something, give something up:

> Er sollte es lieber lassen.   He should give it up.
> Note also the expression
> Laß ihn in Ruhe: Leave him in peace.

§45 IMPERSONAL VERBS

A) Indicating Weather:

> Es regnet.   It is raining.
> Es schneit.   It is snowing.
> Es donnert.   It is thundering.
> Es blitzt.   It is lightning.
> **Note:** frieren, to freeze:
> Es friert.   It is freezing.
> but also Ich friere.   I am freezing.

B) Indicating what someone unknown is doing:

> Es klopft.   There is someone knocking at the door.
> Es klingelt.   There is someone ringing at the door.

C) Indicating general activity:

> Es brennt.   Something's burning, there's a fire.

D) Indicating a state (with dative of person)

> Mir ist kalt/warm.   I am cold/warm.
> Ihm wurde schlecht.   He felt sick.
> Es fehlt ihm an Geduld.   He lacks patience.

> **Note also:** es gefällt mir   I like it.
> This can have another object:
> Der Film gefällt mir.   I like the film.

> Also   Es gelingt mir.   I succeed.

> (For **es ist/es gibt** see §20)

§46 COMMON VERBS + DATIVE

A)

ähneln/gleichen	to resemble
antworten	to answer
danken	to thank
drohen	to threaten
folgen	to follow
gefallen	to please
helfen	to help
trauen	to trust
stehen	to suit

e.g. Das Jackett **steht** dir (gut).

Note: er antwortete **Mir** but er antwortete **auf meine Frage**.

B) Common verbs with *dative of person* and *accusative of thing:*

zeigen	to show	glauben	to believe	sagen	to say
erzählen	to tell	verzeihen	to pardon, excuse,		
forgive	verbieten	to forbid			

     Er glaubt es mir nicht.
     Ich verzeihe dir deine Ungeduld (impatience).
     Er sagt es ihm.
     Er erzählte mir die Geschichte.
     Er zeigt es ihr.
     Ich verbiete es dir.

Note that **glauben** and **verzeihen** can also just have the dative of person:
     Ich glaube ihm.   Verzeihen Sie mir!

§47 VERBS WITH TWO ACCUSATIVE OBJECTS

fragen:	Er fragte mich, was ich meinte.
	He asked me what I thought.
lehren:	Er lehrt ihn die Sprache.
	He teaches him the language.
nennen:	Wir nennen sie Anke.
	We call her Anke.
kosten:	Es kostete mich den gleichen Betrag.
	It cost me the same amount.

§48 THE PRESENT PARTICIPLE

The German present participle is formed by adding **d** to the infinitive:
     weinend   atmend   wandernd   trocknend

It can only be used **(a)** adjectivally:
     die weinenden Kinder   the crying children
     mit fließendem Wasser   with running water

or (**b**) adverbially:

Er ging leise fluchend weiter.   He went on, quietly cursing.
Sie trug ein leuchtend blaues Kleid.   She wore a dazzlingly blue dress.

In other cases the Present Participle, so widely used in English, should be translated by something else.

A) By the Infinitive:

After an adjective:
Es ist schön, hier **zu sein**. = It is nice being here.
Especially after some prepositions:
ohne . . . **zu** + infinitive
ohne ein Wort zu sagen   without saying a word
anstatt . . . **zu** + infinitive
anstatt heute abend zu kommen   instead of coming this evening
and after hören, sehen, bleiben:

Ich hörte ihn lachen.   I heard him laughing.
Ich sah ihn essen.   I saw him eating.
Ich blieb stehen.   I remained standing.

B) By the past participle after **kommen**:

Er kam gelaufen.   He came running.

C) By a phrase with a conjunction:

before going = before he went = bevor er ging
after eating = after he had eaten = nachdem er gegessen hatte
being there = since he was there = da er dort war
getting up = whilst he got up = indem er aufstand

D) By a phrase with relative pronoun (der/die/das):

The man lying there = The man who is lying there = Der Mann, der da liegt

E) By **und** + verb:

He lies there snoring = He lies there and snores = Er liegt da und schnarcht.

F) With the preposition **bei** + verbal noun:

on getting in   beim Einsteigen

§49 TABLE OF MOST COMMON STRONG VERBS

Note 1:   3rd. person *irregular* present tense is given.

Note 2:   Verbs taking **sein** are marked with an asterisk, but remember that verbs normally taking **sein** take **haben** with a direct object (§29e).

INFINITIVE	MEANING	PRESENT	IMPERFECT	PAST PARTICIPLE
backen	to bake		backte	gebacken
befehlen	to give orders	befiehlt	befahl	befohlen
beginnen	to begin		begann	begonnen
beißen	to bite		biß	gebissen
biegen	to turn, bend		bog	gebogen*
bieten	to offer		bot	geboten
binden	to fasten, tie		band	gebunden
bitten	to ask, request		bat	gebeten
blasen	to blow	bläst	blies	geblasen
bleiben	to remain		blieb	geblieben*
braten	to roast, fry	brät	briet	gebraten
brechen	to break	bricht	brach	gebrochen*
brennen	to burn		brannte	gebrannt
bringen	to bring		brachte	gebracht
denken	to think		dachte	gedacht
dürfen	to be allowed to	darf	durfte	gedurft/dürfen
einladen	to invite	lädt ein	lud ein	eingeladen
empfangen	to receive, greet	empfängt	empfing	empfangen
empfehlen	to recommend	empfiehlt	empfahl	empfohlen
erschrecken	to be frightened	erschrickt	erschrak	erschrocken*
essen	to eat	ißt	aß	gegessen
fahren	to drive, ride	fährt	fuhr	gefahren*
fallen	to fall	fällt	fiel	gefallen*
fangen	to catch	fängt	fing	gefangen
finden	to find		fand	gefunden
fliegen	to fly		flog	geflogen*
fliehen	to flee		floh	geflohen*
fließen	to flow		floß	geflossen*
fressen	to eat (of animals)	frißt	fraß	gefressen
frieren	to freeze		fror	gefroren*
geben	to give	gibt	gab	gegeben
gehen	to go		ging	gegangen*
gelingen	to succeed		gelang	gelungen*
gelten	to be valid	gilt	galt	gegolten
genießen	to enjoy		genoß	genossen
geschehen	to happen	geschieht	geschah	geschehen*
gewinnen	to win		gewann	gewonnen
gießen	to pour		goß	gegossen
gleichen	to resemble		glich	geglichen
gleiten	to glide		glitt	geglitten*
graben	to dig	gräbt	grub	gegraben

INFINITIVE	MEANING	PRESENT	IMPERFECT	PAST PARTICIPLE
greifen	to grasp, seize		griff	gegriffen
haben	to have	hat	hatte	gehabt
halten	to hold	hält	hielt	gehalten
hängen	to be hanging		hing	gehangen
heben	to lift, raise		hob	gehoben
heißen	to be called		hieß	geheißen
helfen	to help	hilft	half	geholfen
kennen	to know		kannte	gekannt
klingen	to sound, ring		klang	geklungen
kommen	to come		kam	gekommen*
können	to be able to	kann	konnte	gekonnt/können
kriechen	to crawl		kroch	gekrochen*
laden	to load	lädt	lud	geladen
lassen	to let, allow	läßt	ließ	gelassen
laufen	to run	läuft	lief	gelaufen*
leiden	to suffer		litt	gelitten
leihen	to lend, loan		lieh	geliehen
lesen	to read	liest	las	gelesen
liegen	to be lying		lag	gelegen
lügen	to tell lies		log	gelogen
messen	to measure	mißt	maß	gemessen
mögen	to like to, may	mag	mochte	gemocht/mögen
müssen	to have to	muß	mußte	gemußt/müssen
nehmen	to take	nimmt	nahm	genommen
nennen	to name		nannte	genannt
pfeifen	to whistle		pfiff	gepfiffen
raten	to advise, guess	rät	riet	geraten
reiben	to rub		rieb	gerieben
reißen	to tear, rip		riß	gerissen
reiten	to ride		ritt	geritten*
rennen	to run		rannte	gerannt*
riechen	to smell		roch	gerochen
rufen	to call		rief	gerufen
schaffen[1]	to create		schuf	geschaffen
scheiden	to part, get divorced		schied	geschieden*
scheinen	to shine, seem		schien	geschienen
schelten	to scold, tell off	schilt	schalt	gescholten
schieben	to shove, push		schob	geschoben
schießen	to shoot		schoß	geschossen
schlafen	to sleep	schläft	schlief	geschlafen
schlagen	to hit, strike	schlägt	schlug	geschlagen
schleichen	to creep, move stealthily		schlich	geschlichen*
schließen	to shut, close		schloß	geschlossen

[1] also weak in the sense 'to manage, get (something) done'

INFINITIVE	MEANING	PRESENT	IMPERFECT	PAST PARTICIPLE
schmeißen	to fling		schmiß	geschmissen
schmelzen	to melt	schmilzt	schmolz	geschmolzen*
schneiden	to cut		schnitt	geschnitten
schreiben	to write		schrieb	geschrieben
schreien	to cry out, shout		schrie	geschrie(e)n
schreiten	to stride		schritt	geschritten*
schweigen	to be silent		schwieg	geschwiegen
schwimmen	to swim		schwamm	geschwommen*
schwingen	to swing		schwang	geschwungen
schwören	to swear		schwor	geschworen
sehen	to see	sieht	sah	gesehen
sein	to be	ist	war	gewesen*
senden[2]	to send		sandte	gesandt
singen	to sing		sang	gesungen
sinken	to sink		sank	gesunken*
sitzen	to be sitting		saß	gesessen
sollen	must, should, am to	soll	sollte	gesollt/sollen
sprechen	to speak	spricht	sprach	gesprochen
springen	to jump		sprang	gesprungen*
stechen	to prick, sting	sticht	stach	gestochen
stehen	to stand		stand	gestanden
stehlen	to steal	stiehlt	stahl	gestohlen
steigen	to climb up		stieg	gestiegen*
sterben	to die	stirbt	starb	gestorben*
stinken	to smell bad		stank	gestunken
stoßen	to push, bump	stößt	stieß	gestoßen
streichen	to put on, spread (butter, paint)		strich	gestrichen
streiten	to quarrel		stritt	gestritten
tragen	to carry, wear	trägt	trug	getragen
treffen	to meet, hit	trifft	traf	getroffen
treten	to step, tread	tritt	trat	getreten*
trinken	to drink		trank	getrunken
tun	to do		tat	getan
verbieten	to forbid		verbot	verboten
verderben	to spoil	verdirbt	verdarb	verdorben
vergessen	to forget	vergißt	vergaß	vergessen
verlieren	to lose		verlor	verloren
vermeiden	to avoid		vermied	vermieden
verschwinden	to disappear		verschwand	verschwunden*
verzeihen	to pardon, forgive		verzieh	verziehen
wachsen	to grow	wächst	wuchs	gewachsen*
waschen	to wash	wäscht	wusch	gewaschen
werden	to become	wird	wurde	geworden*
werfen	to throw	wirft	warf	geworfen
wiegen	to weigh		wog	gewogen
wissen	to know	weiß	wußte	gewußt
wollen	to want to	will	wollte	gewollt/wollen
ziehen	to pull		zog	gezogen
zwingen	to force, compel		zwang	gezwungen

[2] also weak in the sense 'to broadcast'

PART FIVE — PREPOSITIONS

§50 PREPOSITIONS ALWAYS + ACCUSATIVE

durch	through → durch den Wald through the wood
ohne	without → ohne mich without me
gegen	against → gegen den Feind against the enemy
wider	against (*feelings*) → wider seinen Willen against his will
um	round → um die Ecke round the corner
für	for → für sie for her
bis	until → bis nächsten Montag until next Monday
entlang	along → die Straße entlang* along the street.

*NB **entlang** usually *follows* noun or pronoun

§51 PREPOSITIONS ALWAYS + DATIVE

mit	with → mit mir with me
nach	after → nach dem Frühstück after breakfast
	according to → nach dem Alphabet alphabetically
von	from → von mir from me
	of (*as alternative to genitive*) → die Frau von meinem Freund the wife of my friend
zu	to (*motion*) → er geht zu ihm/zum Bahnhof/zur Schule He is going to his house/to the station/to school
aus	out of → aus dem Haus out of the house
bei	at the house of, near → bei dir at your house
	during → bei diesem Wetter in this weather
seit	since, for (*time*) → Seit einem Monat wohnen wir hier. We have been living here for a month.
außer	except → alle außer meinem Bruder all except my brother
gegenüber	opposite → der Schule *gegenüber** opposite the school
entgegen	towards → dem Rathaus *entgegen** towards the town hall

*NB **gegenüber** and **entgegen** usually follow the noun

§52 PREPOSITIONS ALWAYS + GENITIVE

trotz	in spite of → trotz des Wetters in spite of the weather
während	during → während des Tages during the day
wegen	because of, on account of → wegen des Geldes because of the money
außerhalb	outside (of) → außerhalb der Tür outside the door
innerhalb	inside (of) → innerhalb des Hauses inside the house
anstatt	instead of → anstatt eines Geschenks instead of a present
um ... willen	for the sake of → um Himmels willen for heaven's sake

§53 PREPOSITIONS + DATIVE OR ACCUSATIVE

A) in and **auf**

in meaning 'into' takes accusative:
Er springt in den See.   He jumps in (to) the lake.
in *not* meaning 'into' takes dative:
Er schwimmt in dem Fluß.   He swims in the river. (*not* into)
Er sitzt in dem Garten.   He sits in the garden. (*not* into)
Similarly 'on' in the sense of 'onto' is auf + accusative:
Er fällt auf den Boden.   He falls on (to) the ground.
If **auf** does *not* mean 'onto', auf takes dative:
Er schläft auf dem Bett.   He sleeps on the bed.
This is because 'into' and 'onto' express *movement* in that direction; the other examples show *position*.

B) Other prepositions take accusative or dative on the same basis, i.e. whether the primary idea is *movement in a particular direction* or *position:*

POSITION → DATIVE   MOVEMENT → ACCUSATIVE
(mnemonic-MAC)

an on, close to, to
Die Uhr hängt an der Wand.
The clock hangs on the wall.
Primary idea POSITION → DATIVE
Er lehnt die Leiter an die Wand.
He leans the ladder on the wall.
Primary idea MOVEMENT → ACCUSATIVE

hinter behind
Sie lag hinter mir.
She was lying behind me.
Primary idea POSITION → DATIVE
Sie ging hinter das Haus.
She went behind the house.
Primary idea MOVEMENT → ACCUSATIVE

neben next to, beside
Er saß neben der Tür.
He was sitting by the door.
Primary idea POSITION → DATIVE
Er setzte sich neben das Fenster.
He sat down beside the window.
Primary idea MOVEMENT → ACCUSATIVE

vor in front of
Vor mir stand ein herrliches Schloß.
In front of me stood a magnificent castle.
Primary idea POSITION → DATIVE
Er stellte es vor das Fenster.
He put it in front of the window.
Primary idea MOVEMENT → ACCUSATIVE

über over
Die Lampe hängt über dem Tisch.
The lamp hangs over the table.
Primary idea POSITION → DATIVE
Der Dieb lief über die Brücke.
The thief ran over the bridge.
Primary idea MOVEMENT → ACCUSATIVE

unter under
Der Videorekorder ist unter dem Fernseher.
The video recorder is under the television set.
Primary idea POSITION → DATIVE
Die Katze kriecht unter den Tisch.
The cat crawls under the table.
Primary idea MOVEMENT → ACCUSATIVE

zwischen between
Das Haus liegt zwischen einem Park und einem Golfplatz.
The house is between a park and a golf course
Primary idea POSITION → DATIVE
Er stellte das Auto zwischen den Bus und das Taxi.
He put the car between the bus and the taxi.
Primary idea MOVEMENT → ACCUSATIVE

Note 1: Do not automatically presume that because a verb of motion is involved, the preposition will be followed by the accusative. For example, one would say:
Sie sprang vor **mir** aus dem Busch.
the stress being on the one position rather than any change of position
Further examples:
Er kam hinter **mir** her.   He was coming along *behind me*.
Er ging neben **ihr**.   He was walking *beside her*.
Er lief zwischen **den beiden**.   He ran *between the two of them*.
(= the three were running together and he was *in the middle*, i.e. no change of relative positions)
BUT
Er lief zwischen **die beiden** = the other two were standing still and he ran between them — change of relative positions

Note 2: Common expressions + dative and accusative

auf dem Land zelten	to camp in the country
aufs Land gehen	to go into the country
an der See sein	to be at the seaside
an die See fahren	to travel to the seaside
im Ausland sein	to be abroad
ins Ausland fahren	to go abroad
im Freien sein	to be outside/in the open
ins Freie gehen	to go outside/into the open air

Note 3: an or auf to translate 'on'?

If the thing (or person) after 'on' is vertical or slanting, or 'on' means' at the side of or 'at', use **an**:

an der Wand (*wall is vertical*)
Sie geht an die Tafel. (*blackboard is vertical*)
am Berg (*on the slope of the hill*)
Frankfurt am Main (= *at the side of the river*)
an der Ecke (= *at the corner*)

If the thing (or person) is horizontal, use **auf**:

auf dem Tisch (*table is horizontal*)
Er fällt auf den Boden. (*floor is horizontal*)

§54 ABBREVIATIONS OF PREPOSITION AND DEFINITE ARTICLE

A) The following combinations are very frequently shortened in both spoken and written German

an dem → am	bei dem → beim	von dem → vom
an das → ans	in dem → im	zu dem → zum
auf das → aufs	in das → ins	zu der → zur

B) Less common abbreviations, normally only heard:

durch das → durchs	unter dem → unterm
für das → fürs	vor dem → vorm
hinter dem → hinterm	vor das → vors

§55 BLENDING OF PREPOSITIONS WITH *DA*

When 'it' and 'them' referring to non-living things are used with prepositions, they are translated by **da-** (or **dar-** before a vowel) and the preposition follows.

Here are some examples (there are others):

daran★	on it, on them	⎫
darauf★	on it, on them	⎪
daraus★	out of it, out of them	⎬ ★r inserted to separate 2 vowels
darin★	in it, in them	⎭
dadurch	through it, through them.	
dafür	for it, for them	
damit	with it, with them	
danach	after it, after them	

Hier ist meine Tasse; daraus trinke ich immer.
Here is my cup; I always drink out of it.
Das ist eine schöne Uhr, aber dafür muß man viel ausgeben.
That is a lovely watch, but one must pay a lot for it.

§56 PREPOSITIONS AFTER CERTAIN VERBS

A) Here are some of the most common verb and preposition combinations:

achten auf + *acc.*   to take notice of
    Du mußt auf die Temperatur achten.
Angst haben vor + *dat.*   to be frightened of
    Ich habe Angst vor Spinnen.
denken an + acc.   to think of/about
    Er denkt immer an seine Freundin.
halten/denken von + *dat.*   to think of (*opinion*)
    Was hältst du von meiner Freundin?
sich erinnern an + *acc.*   to remember
    Ich erinnere mich an den Tag.
es fehlt . . . an + *dat.*   . . . is short of/lacks
    Es fehlt mir an Geld.
sich freuen auf + *acc.*   to look forward to
    Ich freue mich auf die Party.
sich freuen über + *acc.*   to be pleased about
    Ich freue mich über das Geschenk.
glauben an + *acc.*   to believe in
    Ich glaube an Poltergeister.
gratulieren zu + *dat.*   to congratulate on
    Ich gratuliere zum Erfolg (success).
halten für + *acc.*   to consider as
    Ich halte das für blöde (silly).
sich interessieren für + *acc.*   to be interested in
    Er interessiert sich für Musik.
klagen über + *acc.*   to complain about
    Er klagt immer über sein Essen.
leiden an + *dat.*   to suffer from
    Er leidet an einer Erkältung.
passen zu + *dat.*   to suit (go with)
    Das Hemd paßt nicht zum Schlips.
schützen vor + *dat.*   to protect from
    Ein Regenschirm schützt vor dem schlechten Wetter.

stammen aus + *dat.*	to come from
Er stammt aus München.	
sich verlieben in + *acc.*	to fall in love with
Romeo verliebte sich in Julia.	
warnen vor + *dat.*	to warn against
Er warnte mich vor dem Hund.	
warten auf + *acc.*	to wait for
Sie wartet auf ihren Freund.	
weinen vor + *dat.*	to cry for/with
Sie weint vor Freude.	
zeigen auf + *acc.*	to point to/at
Er zeigt auf das Warnschild (warning notice).	
zittern vor + *dat.*	to tremble with
Sie zittert vor Kälte.	

B) Related nouns usually take the same preposition:

Freude über + *acc.* joy at

N.B. Gedanken **über** + *acc.* thoughts about

Glaube an + *acc.* belief in

Schutz vor + *dat.* protectio

from

Warnung vor + *dat.* warni

about

§57 PREPOSITIONS AFTER CERTAIN ADJECTIVES

begierig nach + *dat.*	greedy for	neidisch auf + *acc.*	envious of
beliebt bei + *dat.*	popular with	sicher vor + *dat.*	safe from
eifersüchtig auf + *acc.*	jealous of	stolz auf + *acc.*	proud of
erfreut über + *acc.*	pleased about		

Again nouns follow suit:

Eifersucht/Neid/Stolz auf + *acc.*

§58 VERBS 'DOUBLING UP' BY HAVING A PREFIX AND PREPOSITION

eintreten in + *acc.*	to enter Er tritt ins Zimmer ein.
einsteigen in + *acc.*	to get into Er steigt in den Bus ein.
aussteigen aus + *dat.*	to get out of Er steigt aus dem Zug aus.
vorbeigehen an + *dat.*	to go past Er geht an dem Supermarkt vorbei.
hineingehen in + *acc.*	to go into Er geht ins Haus hinein.
herauskommen aus + *dat.*	to come out of Er kommt aus dem Haus heraus.
aufpassen auf + *acc.*	to attend to, pay attention to Sie paßt auf das Baby auf.

(Further examples of prepositional usage-see Part 7, §60–63)

PART SIX — WORD ORDER

§59 FACTORS AFFECTING WORD ORDER

A) Put the *infinitive* at the *end* of the sentence or clause

Ich beschloß, ein Eis zu **essen.**
Ich beschloß, ein Eis zu **essen**, denn das Wetter war so warm.

B) Put the *past participle* at the *end* also:

Ich habe ein Eis **gegessen.**
What if there is both an infinitive and a past participle at the end?
Which takes precedence?
Ich habe vergessen zu fragen.   is preferred to
Ich habe zu fragen vergessen.   (but either is possible)

C) The relative pronouns **der, die, das** and the following conjunctions send the verb to the end of the sentence or clause (Mnemonic V T E — word sending Verb To End):

der, die, das	who, which (*all cases*)
als	when, at the same time as
auch wenn selbst wenn	} even if
wenn	if, when, whenever
als ob als wenn	} as if (+ *subjunctive*)
bevor ehe	} before
bis	until
da	since, seeing that.
damit	in order that, so that
daß	that
falls	in case
indem	while, whilst
während	while, whilst, whereas
nachdem	after
ob	whether
obgleich obschon obwohl	} although
seit seitdem	} since (*referring to time*)
sobald	as soon as
so daß	so that (= with the result that)
solange	as long as
trotzdem	despite the fact that
weil	because
wie	as, how

Note: the use of commas to divide the clauses.
Der Mann, der an der Ecke steht, wartet auf seine Freundin.
Sie weiß, daß er sie liebt.
Ich erkannte ihn, sobald ich ihn erblickte.

(i) All the question forms (See Section 23) are V T E s when they
introduce an indirect question (i.e. there is usually no question
mark):
Er wußte nicht, wie lange es dauern **würde**.
He didn't know how long it would last.
Do not be fooled by cases where the indirect question is itself part of
a direct question (i.e. there *is* a question mark):

Können Sie mir sagen, wann der Zug einfährt?
    Direct Question   *Indirect Question*
    Can you tell me   when the train comes in?

Wollen Sie mir bitte sagen, warum Sie nicht früher gekommen
sind?
      Direct Question   *Indirect Question*
      Will you please tell me   why you didn't come earlier?

(ii) The V T E is very strong grammatically and overrides other rules of
word order. e.g. *V T E overrides rule (a)* (Infinitive at end):
Ich sage nochmals, daß ich ein Eis essen **möchte**.
(Infinitive **essen** is pushed one place back)
V T E overrides rule (b) (Past Participle at end):
Sobald er das Eis gegessen **hat**,
(Past Participle **gegessen** is pushed one place back)

The only thing grammatically stronger than a V T E is a block of 2
infinitives:
Er wird heute kommen müssen. (*2 infinitives*)
Put V T E in front = Weil er heute **wird** kommen müssen
wird has moved past **heute** but cannot pass the 2 infinitives.

(iii) Note the order in the following sentence:
Die Vase, die auf der Kommode steht, ist sehr wertvoll.
The subordinate clause **die auf der Kommode steht** is introduced
by the relative pronoun **die**, which is a V T E. The V T E, however,
has no influence over the position of the verb in the main clause. Do
not therefore be tempted to send **ist** to the end as well.

D) In indirect speech 'daß' can be omitted. Therefore, instead of:
Er sagte, daß er sehr hungrig sei.
   one can say:
Er sagte, er sei sehr hungrig.

E) **Conjunctions which are not V T E s**

(i) und   — and   denn — for (= because)
    aber   — but   oder — or
    sondern — but (*following* nicht *or* kein)
    are followed by normal order of subject and verb

Ich gehe, und **er kommt** auch.
Ich verreise, aber **du bleibst** hier.

(ii) However note the following:
Weil wir so gute Freunde sind und immer miteinander **umgehen**.
umgehen goes to the end because **weil** is understood in the second
clause (= because we are such good friends and (because) we always
go around together).

F) Separable Prefixes

ab-, an-, auf-, aus-, ein-, fort-, her- and **hin-**
and their combinations (e.g. herauf-, hinunter-), **los-,**
mit-, nach-, nieder-, statt-, vor-, vorbei-, vorüber-,
weg-, zu-, zurück-, zusammen-, weiter-.
Separable Prefixes break away from the verb and go to the end of the
sentence or clause:
Er geht die Straße **hinunter**.
This is true even if the verb is on its own:
Ich komme **mit**.   Komm **mit**!
However, if the sentence or clause begins with a V T E, the prefix and
verb join up again *to form one word*:
Wenn er die Straße **hinuntergeht**, . . .
Note that separable prefixes also do *not* separate from the verb if:
• The verb is an infinitive: Er will **mitkommen**.
• The verb is a past participle: Er ist **mitgekommen**.

Position of **zu** and **ge** with infinitive and past participle having a
separable prefix:
zu goes between prefix and infinitive:
Er entschloß sich aus**zu**gehen.
ge goes between prefix and past participle:
Er ist hinaus**ge**gangen.

G) Inversion of Subject and Verb

If a word or words other than
• a subject
• a V T E
• Ja, Nein, Tja, Na, Ach, Also, etc.
• und, aber, denn, oder, sondern
begin(s) the sentence or clause, subject and verb invert, i.e. change
places. This is the case even if the item which is put first is a whole
clause.
Summarised by Mnemonic:
WOSI (Word(s) Other than Subject → Inversion)
e.g. Auf der Schaukel **sitzt der Junge**.
Eine Stunde später **kommt er** nach Hause.
Leider **ist er** krank.
Jetzt **geht es** los.
Den Wagen **kauft er** morgen.
Weil ich so müde bin, **gehe ich** gleich ins Bett.
Wenn du in die Schule gehst, **komme ich** mit.
,,Komm gut nach Hause", **sagte sie**.

Note 1: Direct speech in inverted commas, as in the last example, counts as a complete clause, so inversion follows, even if there is only one word in direct speech:

„Fabelhaft!" rief der Fan.

Note 2: Do not put a comma after WOSI phrase (as opposed to after a complete clause):

Bald danach verließen wir das Haus.

Note 3: But there is a comma (and *no* inversion) after **Ja**, **Nein**, **Tja**, **Na**, **Ach**, **Also** etc. starting the sentence as statements:

Ja, ich komme gleich.
Na schön, er wird bald kommen.
Also gut, wir gehen morgen.

Note 4: A WOSI after **und**, **aber**, **denn**, **oder** or **sondern** cancels the normal order and causes inversion:

Ich traf ihn **und dann gingen wir** ins Kino.

H) Other cases of inversion

(i) In direct question there is inversion in all cases:

Kommst du?   Gehst du?   Wann kommst du?   Wohin gehst du?

(ii) If the subject and a verb in the imperfect subjunctive are inverted, then this is a conditional or 'if' clause:

Wäre ich Millionär, könnte ich alles kaufen.
If I were a millionaire I could buy everything
(cf. English 'were I a millionaire . . .')

(iii) After **als** + subjunctive meaning 'as if' the verb is also inverted:

Er sah aus, als wäre er krank
He looked as if he were ill
This is an alternative to **als ob** (V T E):
Er sah aus, als ob er krank wäre.

I) Order of Nouns and Pronouns

2 Nouns together — Dative before Accusative:
Er erzählt seiner Schwester die ganze Geschichte.
2 Pronouns together — Accusative before Dative:
Ich gebe es ihm.
Noun + Pronoun — Pronoun first whether Dative or Accusative:
Er schenkt ihr das Buch.
Ich gab es dem Kind.

J) Position of the *reflexive pronoun* is as close to the subject as possible:

Ich will **mich** hier setzen.
Er mußte in die Stadt, obwohl er **sich** zuhause ausruhen wollte.

K) Order of Adverbs and Adverbial Phrases

TIME first — then MANNER — PLACE last
Er geht   immer   langsam   zur Schule
          Time   *Manner*   *Place*

PART SEVEN — NUMBERS, DATES, QUANTITY, TIME

§60 NUMBERS

1 eins	11 elf	21 einundzwanzig	122 hundertzweiundzwanzig
2 zwei	12 zwölf	32 zweiunddreißig	203 zweihundertdrei
3 drei	13 dreizehn	43 dreiundvierzig	314 dreihundertvierzehn
4 vier	14 vierzehn	54 vierundfünfzig	465 vierhundertfünfundsechzig
5 fünf	15 fünfzehn	65 fünfundsechzig	506 fünfhundertsechs
6 sechs	16 sechzehn	76 sechsundsiebzig	617 sechshundertsiebzehn
7 sieben	17 siebzehn	87 siebenundachtzig	888 achthundertachtundachtzig
8 acht	18 achtzehn	98 achtundneunzig	999 neunhundertneunundneunzig
9 neun	19 neunzehn	99 neunundneunzig	1,000 tausend
10 zehn	20 zwanzig	100 hundert	1,001 tausend(und)eins
		101 hunderteins	1,100 tausendeinhundert

Note especially:
spelling of: sechzehn   siebzehn   dreißig   sechzig   siebzig

Numbers are written together as one word except for millions:
   1,400,000 = *eine* Million vierhunderttausend   2,000,000 = zwei
Millionen

ein or **eins**? only with the s in 1, 101, 201, etc., and when a figure on its
own not followed by a noun
   ∴ 1001 Punkte = tausendundein Punkte.
      1,80 Meter = ein Meter achtzig
In giving height, weight etc., where the word **Meter** or **Kilo** is omitted one
would however say e.g.
   Er ist **eins** achtzig (= 1,80 Meter) groß.

The figure 1 in German is written with a tail: *1*
The figure 7 has a line through it to avoid confusion: ⅂

'Once', 'twice' etc. = einmal, zweimal
'For the first time' = zum ersten Mal *or* zum erstenmal.
Buying one *single ticket* = einmal einfach (*bus, train*)

zwo is used instead of **zwei**, especially in situations where confusion with
drei is possible (e.g. on the telephone or when dictating).
Telephone numbers are written in pairs but normally said singly:
   36   39   2 = drei sechs   drei neun   zwo
However many people would say
sechsunddreißig   neununddreißig   zwo

Words for 'number':
   die Zahl   (numeral, figure)
   die Nummer   (house, room, telephone no.)
   die Anzahl   (number of people etc.)

die Ziffer   (numeral, digit)
(e.g. römische Ziffern/arabische Ziffern)
Note also: die Linie 2 = the no. 2 (bus, tram)
Nouns: eine Eins, eine Zwei etc., meaning the written number or school
mark
The plural is used where there is no preceding number:
Hunderte   Tausende
Fractions $\frac{1}{2}$ = Eine Hälfte $\frac{1}{3}$ = ein Drittel $\frac{1}{4}$ = ein Viertel $\frac{1}{5}$ =
ein Fünftel etc.
a sixteenth *of an* inch = ein Sechzehntel Zoll
a quarter *of an* hour = eine Viertelstunde
BUT half a(n) . . . = ein halber/eine halbe/ein halbes . . .
i.e. an *adjective* — eine halbe Stunde
$1\frac{1}{2}$, $2\frac{1}{2}$ etc. = anderthalb *or* eineinhalb, zweieinhalb etc.
Decimal Point in German is a comma:
e.g. 0.9 → 0, 9 (*spoken* null komma neun)
Note: 1 005   2 478 — leave a space after number of thousands
but do *not* put a comma, otherwise = 1.005, 2.478

§61a DATES

Der wievielte ist heute?   What date is it today?
Heute ist der erste/zweite/dritte/sie**bte** (*or* siebente) August.   Today is
the 1st/2nd/3rd/7th August.
Date by itself at the top of a letter etc. is in the accusative:
March 10th = den zehnten März *or* den 10. März *or* den 10.3.
Formation of ordinal numbers:
2nd to 19th add **te** to the number:
Heute ist der neunzehn**te**/19. Mai.   mein siebzehn**ter** Geburtstag
20th onwards add **ste** to the number:
Heute ist der zwanzig**ste**/20. Mai.   das hundert**ste** Mal
'On (the)' with dates = **am**:
Wann haben Sie Geburtstag? **Am** ersten Juni
In 1995 = **im** Jahre 1995   in March = **im** März   in summer = **im** Sommer

§61b AGE

Sie ist schon fünf Jahre alt.   She is already five years old
als ich in deinem Alter war   when I was your age
im Alter von dreißig Jahren/mit dreißig Jahren   at the age of 30

§62 QUANTITY

When expressing a quantity of something, masculine and neuter nouns retain the singular form:
Zwei Glas Bier   Zwei Pfund Bananen
Zwei Stück Kuchen
(but use the plural e.g. zwei **Gläser** if you are thinking of the objects themselves)
The same applies to weights and measures:
drei Kilo   hundert Gramm
zwei Fuß lang/breit/hoch/tief
6,50 Meter = sechs Meter fünfzig
Feminine nouns do take a plural:
zwei Flaschen Wein   drei Tassen Kaffee
Exception here is **die Mark**:
1,50DM = eine Mark fünfzig   8,80DM = acht Mark achtzig
(No dots after D or M)

> **Speed:** 100 Kilometer **in** der Stunde/**pro** Stunde (*abbreviation* km/h)
> Er fuhr **mit** 100 km/h   He drove *at* 100 k.p.h.

§63 TIME

A) *Time of Day* ein Uhr — 1 o'clock   zwei Uhr — 2 o'clock etc.

BUT eine Uhr — a clock, watch   eine Stunde — an hour

B) zwei Uhr fünf *or* fünf (Minuten) nach zwei

acht Uhr vierzig *or* zwanzig (Minuten) vor neun

vier Uhr fünfzehn *or* Viertel nach vier
or Viertel fünf (i.e. $\frac{1}{4}$ of the way to 5)

zehn Uhr dreißig *or* halb elf (i.e. $\frac{1}{2}$ way to 11)

sieben Uhr fünfundvierzig *or* Viertel vor acht
or dreiviertel acht ($\frac{3}{4}$ of the way to 8)

C) 'at' with clock time is **um**: um neun Uhr.

D) '(at) about' with time is **gegen**: gegen neun Uhr
or **um** ... **ungefähr**: um neun Uhr ungefähr

E) The 24 hour clock is used more in official and public situations in Germany, especially in broadcasting and for theatre, concert and church times:

> um zwanzig Uhr = at 8 p.m.

F) Days and times of day

> Use **am** with days → **am** Montag   **am** Freitag
> Also **am** with times of day → **am** Vormittag   **am** Abend
> BUT **in** der Nacht
> **Note: um** Mittag and **um** Mitternacht because these are exact times.
> BUT **zu** Mittag essen   to have lunch
>   **zu** Abend essen   to have an evening meal

G) With **Zeit** use **zu**:

> zu dieser Zeit   at this time

H) With Moment/Augenblick use **in**:

> in diesem Moment/Augenblick   at this moment

I) With festivals use **zu**:

> zu Ostern   at Easter
> zu Weihnachten   at Christmas
> zu Pfingsten   at Whitsun

J) Time — how long + *accusative*:

> Er blieb den ganzen Tag.   He stayed the whole day.
> **Note also:** zwei Stunden lang   for two hours

K) To stress unbroken continuity add **hindurch** ('through'):

> Ich schlief die ganze Nacht hindurch.
> I slept the whole night through.

L) Genitive Constructions

> eines Morgens   one morning   eines Montags   one Monday
> eines Abends   one evening   eines Tages   one day (*future sense*)
> eines Nachts   one night   (*even though* Nacht *is feminine*)

M) Adverbial Constructions (so small letters)

		Of repeated events	
heute morgen	this morning	morgens	in the morning(s)
heute nachmittag	this afternoon	nachmittags	in the afternoon(s)
heute abend	this evening	abends	in the evening(s)
gestern abend	yesterday evening	montags	on Monday(s)
morgen nachmittag	tomorrow afternoon	mittwochs	on Wednesday(s) etc

N) Finally:

morgen früh	tomorrow morning
vorgestern	the day before yesterday
übermorgen	the day after tomorrow
heute vor acht Tagen	a week ago today
heute in acht Tagen	in a week's time
bei Tage/bei Nacht	by day/by night
ab heute/ab neun Uhr	from today/from nine o'clock (onwards)

PART EIGHT — POINTS TO WATCH
(*presented alphabetically*)

§64 *ABER* or *SONDERN* for 'but'?

The usual word is **aber**; after a negative, in most cases, **sondern**. However **sondern** is only used where there is a direct contrast between two alternatives:

Der Film ist nicht in Farbe sondern schwarzweiß.

However in:

Der Film wird dich nicht interessieren, aber komm mit, wenn du willst.

though the word for 'but' does follow a negative the verbs are not alternatives, therefore **aber**.

Note also the expression **nicht nur**...**sondern auch** 'not only...but also.'

§65 *AM HIMMEL* or *IM HIMMEL?*

am Himmel = in the sky
im Himmel = in heaven

§66 ANKOMMEN, ERREICHEN

ankommen = to arrive
Hoffentlich ist er gut angekommen.   I hope he has arrived safely.
ankommen in + *dat.* = to arrive at/in
Er ist eben in der Stadt angekommen.   He has just arrived in town.
erreichen = to reach (*requires direct object*)
Endlich erreichten wir den Fluß.   Finally we reached the river.

§67 *AUF/AB* = up/down

stromauf	upstream	**stromab**	downstream
bergauf	uphill	**bergab**	downhill

§68 *AUFWACHEN* OR *WECKEN?*

aufwachen = to wake up (on one's own)
Ich wachte sehr spät auf.
wecken = to wake (someone else) up
Seine Mutter weckt ihn jeden Morgen.
(cf. der Wecker, alarm clock)

§69 COMMA BEFORE THE INFINITIVE OF THE VERB WITH *ZU?*

No comma in front of the plain infinitive with zu:
Es beginnt zu regnen.
If there is another word before the second verb, which relates to that second verb, insert a comma:
Wir essen, um zu leben.
Er hofft, heute zu kommen.
Sie hat versprochen, die Schuhe zu putzen.
Note: Es beginnt leider zu regnen. (It is unfortunately beginning to rain) has no comma because **leider** does not qualify **regnen**.

§70 COMMA BEFORE *UND* OR *ODER* INTRODUCING A CLAUSE

A comma usually seals off one clause from another (see also §105), but no comma should be inserted where one element is common to both clauses (usually the subject but it can be a verb):
ich arbeite oder ich spiele (*no comma*; ich *common to both*)
sie spielt Tennis und er Fußball (spielt *common to both*)
Otherwise insert a comma:
ich arbeite, und **du** spielst

§71 CONSTRUCTIONS WITH *HABEN*

Angst haben   to be frightened/anxious
Durst haben   to be thirsty
Hunger haben   to be hungry
Glück haben   to be lucky
Pech haben   to be unlucky
Lust haben   to wish, fancy
recht haben   to be right

unrecht haben   to be wrong
Ich habe Lust, ein heißes Würstchen zu essen.
I fancy eating a hot dog.

§72 *DER, DIE, DAS* — DIFFERENT MEANINGS/USES

A) the definite article 'the'

> N.B. used also with parts of the body and clothing where we would use the possessive adjective:
> Er steckte **die** Hand in **die** Tasche.
> He stuck his hand in his pocket.

B) 'the one', 'the ones'

> Welcher gefällt Ihnen am besten? — Der im Schaufenster.
> Which one do you like best? — The one in the window.
> Similarly used as the emphatic alternative to **er**, **sie**, **es** for 'he', 'she', 'it', 'these/those':
> Der kann aber singen!   He can certainly sing!
> Die sind schön!   These are nice!

C) The relative pronoun 'who', 'which' (V T E)

> Da wohnt eine Frau, **die** ein richtiges Klatschmaul ist.
> A woman lives there who is a real gossip.

§73 *DA* — DIFFERENT MEANINGS

A) 'there'

> Wer ist da?   Who's there?
> **Note also:**
> Da komme ich nicht mit.   I'm not with you there.
> (i.e. I don't understand)

B) 'here'

> Da bin ich!   Here I am!

C) 'then'

> Da sagte er...   Then he said...

D) 'then' (= in that case)

> Da komme ich gleich zurück.
> Then I'll come back straight away.

E) 'as,' 'seeing that' (conjunction, V T E)

    Da es so warm ist, essen wir heute draußen.
    As it is so warm we'll eat outside today.

§74 *DAMIT, UM...ZU, SO DAß*

damit = 'so that' (*expressing purpose*), 'in order that'
    Ich werde babysitten, damit du deine Freundin besuchen kannst.
    I shall babysit so that you can visit your friend.

um...zu also expresses purpose but means 'in order *to*'
    Ich werde babysitten, um etwas Geld zu verdienen.
    I'll babysit to earn some money.

Note also use of **um...zu**

(i) after **genug** (enough):
    Du bist nicht alt genug, **um** alleine zu gehen.
(ii) after **zu** = 'too' + infinitive:
    Es ist zu früh, **um** ins Bett zu gehen.

so daß = 'so that,' 'with the result that'
    Er war krank, so daß er im Bett bleiben mußte.
    He was ill so he had to stay in bed.

§75 *DANN* OR *DENN?*

    dann = then, after that
    denn = for, because
But note idiomatic use of **denn**:
    Was ist denn los?   What's up then?

§76 *DAS* OR *DAß?* (TRANSLATING 'THAT')

Remember **daß** *never* means 'which'
                  never means 'it'
    He said that he would come.
'that' cannot mean 'which', therefore **daß**:
    Er sagte, daß er kommen würde.

    The book that he gave me...
'that' can mean 'which', therefore not **daß**:
    Das Buch, das er mir schenkte...

Similarly: That's nice; I like that.
'that' means 'it', therefore not **daß**:
Das ist schön; ich habe das gern.

§77 *DERSELBE, DIESELBE, DASSELBE*

is written as one word in all cases and genders, singular and plural, but
takes endings as if written separately:
   an de**m**selb**en** Tag   on the same day

§78 *DÜRFEN, ERLAUBEN*

dürfen = to be allowed to
Er darf kommen.   He is allowed to come.
erlauben + *dat.* = to allow, permit
Seine Frau erlaubt ihm nicht, daß er mit seinen Freunden ausgeht.
Of course both verbs can be used to express the same idea:
Man erlaubt ihm zu kommen.
Seine Frau sagt, er darf nicht mit seinen Freunden ausgehen.

§79 *EBEN* AND *SOGAR*

eben means 'even' only as an adjective in the sense of 'level':
Der Boden ist eben.   The ground is level.

As an adverb **eben** usually means 'just':
Er ist eben verreist.   He's just gone away.
sogar is 'even' in the sense — would you believe it?
Sogar Oma kam.   Even grandma came.
sogar is therefore always an adverb.

§80 *ERST* OR *NUR* FOR 'ONLY'?

Use **erst** when time is involved:
Er kommt erst um zwei Uhr.
He's only coming at two o'clock (i.e. not until two o'clock).
Otherwise **nur**:
Ich hab nur zwei Mark übrig.
I've only 2 marks left.

§81 *ETWAS* OR *EINIGE*?

etwas = 'some' with *singular* noun:
etwas Milch, etwas Zeit
einige = 'some' with *plural* noun:
einige Menschen
Note also: ein paar (invariable) = a few, a couple

§82 *FRAGEN* OR *BITTEN*?

fragen nach = to ask about, enquire after
bitten um = to ask for, request
Both verbs take the accusative of the person
Ich fragte ihn nach seiner Frau.   I asked him about his wife.
Ich bat ihn um Feuer.   I asked him for a light.
Note: eine Frage **stellen** = to ask a question

§83 *GERN HABEN* OR OTHER VERB + *GERN*?

gern haben = to like someone or something
Ich habe ihn gern.   Ich habe Sauerkraut gern.
other verb + **gern** = to like doing something
Ich schwimme gern.   Ich tanze gern.

§84 *HEIßEN* OR *NENNEN*?

heißen = to be called; to mean
Er heißt Georg Schwarz.   Was heißt 'blöde' auf englisch?
nennen = to call, name
Ich nenne ihn Willi.   I call him Willi.
Das nenne ich eine Frechheit!   I call that cheek!

§85 *HIER* OR *HIERHER*? ETC.

Position here = **hier**   there = **dort/da**
Er steht hier.   Sie liegt dort/da.
Movement here = **hierher**   there = **dorthin/dahin.** (old English 'hither'
or
'thither')
Komm hierher!   Gehen Sie dahin/dorthin!

§86 PREFIXES *HIN* AND *HER*

her has the sense of 'towards'
hin has the sense of 'away from'
so one usually finds **her** with **kommen**
        hin with **gehen**
Er kommt herein. Komm raus! (*short for* heraus)
Imagine you are *in* a swimming pool and tell your friend to jump in. You
would say
 Spring **her**ein!
But if you are standing on the side with your friend you would say
 Spring **hin**ein!
Imagine your friend and yourself are at the top of a hill. You tell your
friend to run down. You would say
 Lauf hinunter!

Note also the following:
 zur Tür herein ⎱ zum Fenster herein ⎱
    hinein ⎰   hinein ⎰
 in through the door/window
 zur Tür heraus ⎱ zum Fenster heraus ⎱
    hinaus ⎰   hinaus ⎰
 out through the door/window

 herauf   = up (towards)
 hinauf   = up (away from)
 herunter/herab = down (towards)
 hinunter/hinab = down (away from)
Note a contradiction to the rule (and rather rude):
Raus! Get out!

§87 *HINTER* OR *HINTEN*? etc.

hinter, über, unter, vor are prepositions and are followed by a noun or
pronoun:
 Der Betrunkene schläft unter dem Tisch.
hinten, oben, unten, vorne are adverbs of place and stand on their own:
 Der Keller ist unten.
 Oben sind drei Schlafzimmer.

§88 *HOCH* AS INFLECTED ADJECTIVE

hoch drops the 'c' if it takes an adjective ending:
Da steht ein **hoher** Turm.

§89 *JETZT* OR *NUN*?

jetzt is now, the present moment, often as opposed to what used to be the case:
Du mußt jetzt ins Bett!   Jetzt kommt er nicht mehr zu uns.
nun is more general, = 'in these circumstances' or 'meanwhile':
Was machen wir nun?   Es war nun Abend geworden.
However, in many cases either will do.

Note: nun can also act as a 'filling-in' word where a speaker pauses or
wants to introduce something:
Nun also ...   Well then ...
Nun, was meinst du?   Now what do you think?

§90 *KEIN* OR *NICHT EIN*?

kein = 'not a,' 'not any':
Er ist kein Freund von mir.
He is not a friend of mine.
Only use **nicht ein** where there is strong emphasis ('not *one*')
Er hat nicht einen Pfennig bezahlt.
He hasn't paid a penny.

§91 *KENNEN* OR *WISSEN*?

kennen = to know, be acquainted with a person or a place or a book etc.
Ich kenne ihn.   Ich kenne Berlin.   Ich kenne das Buch.
wissen = to know a fact, know that ..., whether ..., how to ...
Ich weiß es. Ich weiß, daß er kommt.
Er weiß sich einzuschmeicheln.   He knows how to ingratiate himself.

§92 *KONNTE* OR *KÖNNTE* = 'COULD'?

konnte refers to the past and is a statement of fact:
Ich konnte es tun.   I could/was able to do it.
könnte refers to the future and is conditional (what would be possible):
Ich könnte es morgen tun.   I could do it tomorrow.

§93 *LASSEN* OR *VERLASSEN*?

lassen = to leave something somewhere:
Kann ich die Tasche hier lassen?   Can I leave the bag here?
verlassen = to leave (quit) a place
Er verläßt das Gebäude.   He is leaving the building.

§94 LETTER WRITING (PERSONAL)

A) Note exclamation mark as alternative to a comma:

Lieber Herr Schmidt!   Liebe Familie Weiß!
If you use an exclamation mark the letter proper starts with a capital;
after a comma use a small letter to begin.

B) In letters all words for 'you' and 'your' have capital letters at all times:

	YOU		*YOUR*	
Du	Dich	Dir	Dein	(1 CAFF)
Ihr	Euch	Euch	Euer	(2 CAFF)
Sie	Sie	Ihnen	Ihr	(NON — CAFF)

C) Conclusion of a personal letter must also follow CAFF rule and have a
capital letter:

Dein/Euer/Ihr   Deine/Eure/Ihre
    John   *Anna*

§95 *LIEGEN*, *LEGEN* OR *SICH HINLEGEN*?

liegen (*strong verb*) = to be lying
Sie liegt auf dem Sofa.
legen (*weak verb*) = to put down (horizontally)
Ich lege das Buch auf den Tisch.
sich hinlegen (*weak verb*) = to lie down
Leg dich hin!

§96 *MEHR* OR *MEHRERE*?

mehr = more — never adds endings
mehr Salz   mit mehr Glück als Verstand
mehrere = several — endings change according to case
Sie hat mehrere Freunde.
Ich machte einen Ausflug mit mehreren Kollegen.

§97 *NACH HAUSE* OR *ZU HAUSE/ZUHAUSE?*

nach Hause = *to* one's home
Wir gehen nach Hause.
zu Hause/zuhause = *at* home
Mutti ist zuhause.

§98 *NOCH* OR *DOCH?*

noch = 'still' referring to *time*:
Er ist noch im Büro.
doch = 'still, yet' in the sense of 'but':
Er ist arm, doch glücklich.
Not also use of **doch** for 'yes' when answer 'no' is expected:
Kommst du nicht? — Doch!

§99 *NOCH EIN* OR *EIN ANDERES?*

noch ein = one more, another (*of the same kind*)
Noch ein Glas Bier?
ein anderes = another (*different*)
Ich möchte ein anderes Glas.
I would like another (different) glass.

§100 *OBEN* OR *NACH OBEN? UNTEN* OR *NACH UNTEN?*

If primarily position is stressed — **oben/unten**:
Er ist oben.   He is upstairs.
Er ist unten.   He is downstairs.
If movement upwards or downwards is involved — **nach oben/nach unten**:
Er geht nach oben.   He goes upstairs.
Er geht nach unten.   He goes downstairs.

§101 *OFFEN* OR *ÖFFNEN? TROCKEN* OR *TROCKNEN?*

offen = open — *adjective:*   Das Fenster ist offen.
öffnen = to open — *verb:*   Das Fenster wird geöffnet.
The window is opened.

Similarly
trocken = dry — *adjective*:   Das Gras ist trocken.
trocknen = to dry — *verb*:   Der Wind trocknet das Gras.

§102 OMISSION OF INDEFINITE ARTICLE

The article is omitted after **sein** and **werden** with occupation, religion and nationality:
Er wird Ingenieur.   Sie ist Protestantin.   Sein Onkel ist Amerikaner.

§103 POSITION OF *NICHT*

A) *before* infinitive, past participle, separated prefix, verb sent to the end or an adjective on its own (predicative adj.):

Er will es nicht kaufen. (*before infinitive*)
Sie hat es nicht gekauft. (*before past participle*)
Er kommt nicht herein. (*before separated prefix*)
Wenn sie nicht kommt. (*before verb sent to the end*)
Er ist nicht klein. (*before predicative adjective*)
(but note: Klein ist er nicht. is also possible)

B) *after* the pronoun

Er mag mich nicht.   Er gab es mir nicht.
Ich sehe dich nicht.   Sag es ihr nicht.
Bild es dir nicht ein (don't imagine).
Laß ihn nicht herein.

C) If a particular word is to be negatively stressed the position of **nicht** varies.

Ich will heute nicht kommen.
This is the normal order; no particular stress.
BUT
Ich will nicht **heute** kommen.   I don't want to come *today*
Ich **will** nicht heute kommen.   I *don't want to* come today
The difference in meaning between the last two examples is conveyed by the intonation of the voice.

§104 PREPOSITION WITH *DA(R)* OR PREPOSITION WITH *WOR*?

da + *preposition* = it *or* them (*inanimate objects*)
wo + *preposition* = which

e.g.	damit	with it/with them	womit	with which
	darauf	on it/on them	worauf	on which
	daraus	out of it/out of them	woraus	out of which
	darin	in it/in them	worin	in which

§105 PUNCTUATION

A) Comma

In English the comma generally indicates a pause and there are cases where it is not really wrong to use one or leave it out. In German the comma is mostly an important aspect of grammar, a grammatical 'sealing off' of clauses and *must not be omitted*.

Der Mann, | der im Garten arbeitet | ,ist mein Vater.

The words in the box form a relative clause and are grammatically sealed off by the commas.
(for use of commas see also §59(c), §69, §70)

B) Inverted Commas (Speech Marks)
Remember by mnemonic:
99 on the line
66 above
e.g. ,,Tschüs" ("Cheerio", "Bye")

C) Colon

In German the colon is often used to introduce Direct Speech:
        Er fragte: ,,Was macht das?"
Note: the colon is followed by a capital letter.

§106 *SAGEN, SPRECHEN, ERZÄHLEN*

sagen = to say something to someone, to tell someone something
Das darfst du (ihm) nicht sagen.
You mustn't say that (to him).
Könnten Sie mir bitte sagen, wie ich zum Fundbüro komme?
Could you please tell me how to get to the lost property office?
sprechen = to speak, talk
Er spricht mit seinem Klassenlehrer.
He is talking to his form teacher.
erzählen = to tell, relate
Erzähl mir die ganze Geschichte!
Tell me the whole story.

§107 *SATT*

Ich **bin** satt. = I'm full up (I've had enough to eat).
Ich **habe ihn** satt. = I'm fed up with him.
Ich **habe es** satt. = I'm fed up with it.

§108 TENSE USED WITH *SEIT*

Ich **studiere** seit drei Jahren.
I *have been* studying for three years.
The present tense is used as the action is still continuing; similarly:
Ich **lernte** die Sprache seit drei Jahren.
I *had been* learning the language for three years.
(*and was still learning it* — therefore the imperfect tense)

§109 *SITZEN* OR *SICH SETZEN*?

sitzen (*strong verb*) = to be sitting
Er sitzt ruhig da.
sich setzen (*weak verb*) = to sit down
Setz dich auf den Sessel.

§110 *ß* OR *SS*?

Use **ß** • at the end of a word (whether part of a compound or not):
Schuß   Schußfeld
     • before letter **t**:   ißt   mußte
     • after a long vowel: Straße
Do not use **ß** after a short vowel in the middle of a word (e.g. müssen).
Note therefore: der Fluß but des Flusses

§111 *SUCHEN, BESUCHEN, VERSUCHEN*

suchen = to look for
besuchen = to visit, attend
(Er besucht die Schule. He attends school.)
versuchen = to try

§112 VERB WITH PREFIX, VERB WITH PREPOSITION

Do not confuse a verb with a prefix (e.g. aufsehen = to look up) with a verb
with a preposition (e.g. sehen auf + *acc.* = to look at).
aufsehen — **auf** is a separable prefix and goes to the end
Sie sieht selten auf.   She seldom looks up.
sehen auf + *acc.* — **auf** is a preposition:
Er sieht auf die Uhr.   He looks at the clock.

§113 *VIEL* OR *VIELE?*

viel = much. It can decline but normally does not:
Mit viel Geld kann man viel erreichen.
viele = many (*plural*). Always declines:
Die Frau kam mit vielen Kindern.

§114 *WAS FÜR EIN* = WHAT KIND OF A ...?

In this phrase **für** is not necessarily followed by the accusative case. The
case of **ein** depends on its noun's role in the sentence:
Was für ein Tag ist es? (*nominative*)
Was für ein**en** Tag haben Sie gehabt? (*accusative*)
Mit was für ein**em** Auto fährt er? (*dative after* mit)

§115 *WENIG, WENIGER, WENIGE*

wenig means 'little', 'not much', and is indeclinable:
Ich habe wenig Geld übrig.
I have little money left.
weniger means 'less' and is also indeclinable:
Ich habe weniger Freizeit als du.
I have less free time than you.
wenige (*plural*) means 'few' and declines:
Sie hat wenige Freundinnen.
She has few friends.

§116 *WOHIN* AND *WORIN*

wohin = whither, where (to):
Wohin gehst du?   Where are you going?
worin = in which/what:
Worin liegt der Unterschied?   Where (= in what) is the difference?

§117 *WOHL*

Meaning:
- well (*in health*):   Ich fühle mich wohl.
- probably: Das ist wohl das beste.
- indeed: Du kannst wohl lachen!

§118 *ZU* BEFORE INFINITIVE?

A) No **zu**
- after modal verbs:
  Er will/mag/muß/soll Tennis spielen.
- after helfen, lehren, lernen, kommen, gehen:

Er hilft mir suchen	He helps me to search
Er lehrt mich schwimmen	He teaches me to swim
Er lernt schwimmen	He learns to swim
Er kommt/geht schwimmen	He comes/goes swimming

But in the first three cases if anything accompanies the infinitive then add **zu**: sie half mir, nach den Juwelen zu suchen

B) Use **zu** if an infinitive is dependent on a verb other than those listed above, on an adjective or on a noun:

e.g. Es beginnt zu regnen   It's beginning to rain
Sie versucht, alles zu tun   She tries to do everything
Er entschloß sich, noch einen Tag zu warten
He decided to wait another day
Es ist möglich, das zu tun   It's possible to do that
Hast du Zeit, ein Glas Wein zu trinken?
Have you time to drink a glass of wine?

PART NINE — VERBS IN CONTEXT

§119 CATCH

(ball, fish etc.) → **fangen**
Der Junge fängt den Ball.
(someone) → **fassen**
Der Schupo faßte den Dieb.
(train, bus etc.) → **erreichen**
Der Schüler erreichte den Bus.
— sight of → **erblicken**
Plötzlich erblickte sie ihren Freund.

§120 CHANGE

(clothes) → **sich umziehen**
Zieh dich um!
(buses, trains etc.) → **umsteigen**
Alles umsteigen!
= alter (*transitive*) → **ändern**
Er änderte seine Pläne.
(*intransitive*) → **sich ändern**
Alles hat sich geändert.
(money) → **wechseln**
In der Wechselstube kannst du das
Geld wechseln.

§121 GET

= become → **werden**
Er wird alt.   Es wird dunkel.
= obtain, receive → **erhalten, bekommen**
Er hat den Scheck erhalten.
or in colloquial speech → **kriegen**
Ich hab' den Ring zum Geburtstag
gekriegt.
= procure, buy → **besorgen**
Willst du mir Brot besorgen?
— into a situation/state → **geraten** (+ sein)
Er ist in Schwierigkeiten geraten.
He has got into difficulties.

§122 GO

on foot	→ **gehen**
Sie geht zur Post.	
by vehicle (including bicycle)	→ **fahren**
Wir fahren nach Berlin.	
— for a walk	→ **spazierengehen** (*separable*)
Sie gingen im Wald spazieren.	
— for a drive	→ **spazierenfahren** (*separable*)
Wir fahren gern sonntags spazieren.	
— for a trip	→ **einen Ausflug machen**
Machen wir einen Ausflug in die Berge!	
= leave, depart on a journey	→ **abfahren**
Wann fährt der Zug ab?	
= take one's leave	→ **sich verabschieden** (*inseparable*)
Ich muß mich jetzt verabschieden. (*or simply* Ich muß jetzt gehen.)	

§123 LOOK

somewhere	→ **sehen** (*colloquial* schauen/gucken)
Sie sah (schaute/guckte) durch das Fenster	
quick look, = glance	→ **blicken**
Sie blickte in meine Richtung.	
= have appearance	→ **aussehen**
Du siehst aber krank aus!	
— at	→ **ansehen** (*separable*)
Sie sah mich an	
— at, = examine	→ **untersuchen**
Der Arzt untersuchte jeden Patienten.	
— round	→ **sich umsehen** (*separable*)
Er sah sich im Geschäft um.	
— round, = view	→ **besichtigen**
Die Touristen besichtigten die Burg.	

§124 MISS

(person)	→ **vermissen**
Ich habe dich sehr vermißt.	
(train etc., opportunity)	→ **verpassen**
Ich habe den Bus verpaßt.	
= fail to notice	→ **verfehlen**
Ich verfehlte die Ausfahrt (*turn off*).	

§125 ORDER

= command, give orders	→ **befehlen** (+ *dat.*)
Er befahl mir, hierher zu kommen.	
(meal, goods, taxi)	→ **bestellen**
Sie bestellte ein Steak.	

§126 PASS

= go past	→ **vorbeigehen/vorbeifahren** (an + *dat.*)
Wir gingen/fuhren an ihm vorbei.	
= overtake	→ **überholen** (*inseparable*)
Das Auto überholte den Lastwagen.	
(of time)	→ **vergehen**
Die Zeit vergeht schnell in den Ferien.	
— an exam	→ **bestehen**
Jeder hat das Examen bestanden.	
= hand over	→ **reichen**
Reichen Sie mir ein Messer bitte.	

§127 PUT

horizontally	→ **legen**
Sie legt den Bleistift auf das Pult.	
vertically	→ **stellen**
Er stellt die Vase auf das Regal. (*shelf*)	
into something else	→ **stecken**
Er steckt das Bonbon in den Mund.	
— on (hat)	→ **aufsetzen**
Sie setzt den neuen Hut auf.	
— on (clothes)	→ **anziehen**
Er zieht einen Anorak an.	

§128 SPEND

— time	→ **verbringen**
Wir haben den Urlaub in den Bergen verbracht.	
— money	→ **ausgeben**
Sie ist sehr freigebig; sie gibt viel Geld aus.	

§129 STOP

of vehicles	→ **halten**
Der Bus hält.	
of a person	→ **stehenbleiben**
Die Dame blieb vor dem Kaufhaus	
stehen.	
= cease	→ **aufhören**
Der Regen hört jetzt auf.	
= make an end (e.g. writing a	→ **Schluß machen**
letter)	
Ich muß jetzt Schluß machen.	
= remain, stay	→ **bleiben**
Er blieb zwei Stunden.	
= reside	→ **sich aufhalten**
Wir hielten uns in einem schönen	
Hotel auf.	
= overnight	→ **übernachten**
Wir haben in einer Jugendherberge	
übernachtet.	
= make stop	→ **anhalten**
Der Polizist hielt den Wagen an.	
= not do	→ **aufhören mit**
Hör auf mit dem Lärm!	
= prevent	→ **verhindern**
Kannst du es nicht verhindern?	

§130 TAKE

train, seat etc.	→ **nehmen**
Ich nehme den Zug. Nehmen Sie	
bitte Platz.	
— an exam	→ **machen**
Machst du Abitur (approx. = A Level)?	
someone somewhere	→ **führen/bringen**
Der Junge führte/brachte den	
Blinden über die Straße.	
= accept	→ **annehmen**
Nehmen Sie dieses kleine Geschenk	
an.	
— a photo	→ **eine Aufnahme machen**
— off (clothes)	→ **ablegen/ausziehen**
Leg den Mantel ab!	
Er zog die Socken aus.	

PART TEN — HINTS ON TRANSLATION OF PARTICULAR WORDS

§131 AFTER

— to decide whether the word is **nachher** (*adverb*)
                               nachdem (*conjunction*)
                               nach (*preposition* + *dat.*)
ask yourself the following:

A) Does 'after' mean 'afterwards'? If so, **nachher**:

Nachher gingen wir nach Hause.

B) If the word 'after' is removed from the sentence, are two separate sentences then created? If so 'after' is a conjunction, ∴ **nachdem**:

Nachdem wir den Strand erreicht hatten, sonnten wir uns.
After we had reached the beach, we sunbathed. (remove 'after' and you are left with two separate sentences: We had reached the beach. We sunbathed.)

C) If neither A nor B applies, then **nach**:

Er schlief **nach** dem Mittagessen ein.

§132 BEFORE

Proceed as above: **vorher** *or* **zuvor** (*adverb*) = beforehand
                         bevor *or* **ehe** (*conjunctions*)
                         vor (*preposition* + *dat. or acc.*)

A) Er hat es nicht **vorher** gelesen. Am Abend **zuvor** kam er zu mir.

B) **Bevor** wir das Kino erreichten, regnete es in Strömen.

C) **Vor** der Party backte sie eine Geburtstagstorte.

§133 AGO

vor + dative.
vor einer Minute   a minute ago   vor zwei Tagen/Jahren   two days/years ago
Note also:
Das ist schon lange her.   That was a long time ago.

§134 BE LATE

A) of people → **spät kommen**
Du kommst immer spät.

B) of buses, trains etc. → **Verspätung haben**
Der Bus hat zehn Minuten Verspätung.

§135 GO/CARRY ON

... doing something = **etwas weitermachen**:
Er ging weiter.   He went on (his way).
Sie las weiter.   She went on reading.
Sie spielten weiter. They carried on playing.

§136 TO DECIDE

A) to resolve (after due consideration) → **beschließen**

Da der Tag so schön war, beschloß er, die Schule zu schwänzen.
As the day was so nice, he decided to play truant from school.
Especially of a meeting or other group of people:
Der Bundestag hat die Erhöhung der Steuern beschlossen.
The Bundestag decided to increase taxes.

B) to make up one's mind → **sich entschließen**

Er kann sich niemals entschließen, was er tun soll.
He can never decide what to do.

C) to come to a decision (especially between several possibilities) → **sich entscheiden**

Er hat sich entschieden, im Ausland zu arbeiten.
He has decided to work abroad.
Sie entschied sich für das rote.
She decided on the red one.

§137 TO ENJOY

A) to enjoy something: Turn the sentence round and use **gefallen** + dative ('to please').

I am enjoying the programme =
Das Programm gefällt mir
(or more colloquially) macht mir Spaß

B) to enjoy food: Use **schmecken** ('to taste good').

Again turn the sentence round:
Die Suppe schmeckte mir.   I enjoyed the soup.

C) to enjoy oneself: **sich unterhalten, sich amüsieren.**

Er unterhält sich auf Urlaub.
He enjoys himself on holiday.
(**Note: sich unterhalten** also means 'to talk, converse')

§138 FINISH

A) finish doing something → **etwas zu Ende tun**

Sie las das Buch zu Ende.
She finished reading the book.

B) be finished with something → **mit etwas fertig sein**

Ich bin mit der Arbeit fertig.   I have finished the work.

C) be finished with somebody → **mit jemandem fertig sein**

Ich bin mit ihm fertig!
I'm finished (through) with him!

§139 TRANSLATING 'IN', 'AT', 'ON' WITH THE FOLLOWING

auf der Straße	in/on the street	auf der Uni	at university
in der Schule	at school	auf der Welt	in the world
auf der Post	at the post office	auf seinem Zimmer	in his room
am Bahnhof	at the station		

§140 LIKE, PREFER AND BEST OF ALL

A) to like doing something: use *verb* + **gern.**
Ich esse gern.   I like eating

B) to prefer doing something: use *verb* + lieber
Ich schlafe lieber.   I prefer to sleep.

C) to like something best of all: use *verb* + am liebsten
Ich sehe am liebsten fern.   I like watching television best.

§141 NEAR, NEARBY

A) *adjective* — **nah(e)**:
der nahe See   the nearby lake   Rettung ist nah.   Help is at hand.

B) *preposition* — **nahe** (bei): nahe (bei) den Geschäften   near the shops
with towns — bei: bei Köln   near Cologne

C) *adverb* — **in der Nähe**: Ist eine Haltestelle in der Nähe?
Is there a stop near (here)?

§142 'TO' WITH TOWNS COUNTRIES AND BUILDINGS

A) *with towns* — **nach**: nach London   nach Düsseldorf

B) *with countries* — **nach** (or **in**, if the country is feminine or plural): nach Holland   nach Frankreich
BUT **in** die Schweiz   in die Türkei   in die USA.

C) *with buildings* — **zu**: zum Bahnhof   zur Schule

§143 TRAVEL 'BY' OR 'ON'

mit dem Wagen	by car	mit dem Schiff	by sea
mit der Straßenbahn	by tram	mit dem Fahrrad	on a bicycle
mit der Bahn	by rail	zu Fuß	on foot
mit der Seilbahn	by cable car	zu Pferde	on horseback

§144 'WHAT' TRANSLATED BY *WIE, WELCHER*

'What' on its own is **was** with the following exceptions:
Wie ist Ihr Name? ⎫
Wie heißen Sie? ⎬ What is your name?
Wie ist Ihre Adresse?   What is your address?
Wie ist Ihre Telefonnummer?   What is your telephone number?
'What' followed by a noun (= 'which') is **welcher, welche, welches**:

Welcher Junge?   What boy?
Welche Farbe hat Ihr Teppich?   What colour is your carpet?
Welches Buch haben Sie?   What book have you got?

§145 WHEN

A) wann for direct and indirect *questions*:

> Wann kommst du uns besuchen?
> Er fragte, wann ich gehen könnte.

B) wenn

> **(i)** 'when (ever)', i.e. with an action or thought which recurs:
> Wenn der Wecker nicht läutete, verschlief er sich.
> Whenever the alarm didn't ring he overslept.
> Wenn wir auf das Land fahren, machen wir gewöhnlich Picknick.
> When we go into the country we usually have a picnic.

> **(ii)** with future events:
> Wenn er kommt, gehen wir spazieren.
> When he comes we'll go for a walk.

C) als describes one particular incident in the past:

> Als der Dieb die Uhr stehlen wollte, erwischte ihn die Aufsicht.
> When the thief tried to steal the watch, the shopwalker caught him.
> Als ich das Dorf erreichte, hörte der Regen plötzlich auf.
> When I reached the village the rain suddenly stopped.

§146 WHILE, WHILST

A) indem *same* subject in both clauses; action of short duration:

> Indem er das sagte, winkte er mit der Hand.

B) während

> **(i)** *same* subject in both clauses; action of longer duration:
> Während sie kocht, trägt sie eine Schürze (apron).

> **(ii)** always to be used with *different* subjects in the two clauses:
> Während **ich** die Zeitung las, sah **sie** fern.

INDEX

The numbers refer to sections